The Grandfath
Owner's Repair Manual

By D. Rod Lloyd

Step by Step
No Prior Experience Required

The following books by D. Rod Lloyd are also available.

The Clock Repairer's Bench Manual: Everything you need to know when repairing mechanical clocks
The Cuckoo Clock Owner's Repair Manual: Step by Step, No Prior Experience Required
The Grandfather Clock Owner's Repair Manual
Happy Anniversary Clock's: 400-Day Owners Repair Manual
A Walk in my Shoes, Biography
The Atmos Clock Repairer's Bench Manual Step by Step
My Clock Won't Run Beginners guide to clock repair

Handbell Ringers Bible
Handbell Ringers Bible Book 2: For the Beginner Handbell Ringer
Build Your own Handbell Tree From Off the Shelf Parts

Laundromat Operations & Maintenance Manual
Money from Mobiles: Mobile Flipping, Loans, Parks, Rentals- A gateway to Real Estate Investing
How to re-hair your Violin, Viola, Cello, or Bass bow
Laundromat Operations & Maintenance Manual
Frederick II - Classic English Narrowboat: A unique Tug / Dutch Barge with a Charming Interior
British to American Dictionary: For Travelers and those who talk to Brits

Home Inspection and Mold Testing Business by an Old Pro
House Flipping for Big Profits by an Old Pro
10% interest
Profitable Rental Property Investing: & House Flipping
How to get rid of MOLD - a homeowner guide
The Care and Feeding of Economy Rental Property by an Old Pro
Toilet Repair or Replacement Without calling a Plumber
Instant Hot Water
To Make End$ Meet: How Not To Be Poor
Around the World with a Twist cruise blog

Contents

Copyright

©

ClockWatchBooks.com

D. Rod Lloyd 2023

First Published 7/14/2019

Introduction

There are many excellent books written for the horologist, apprentice, or professional clock shop, but this book is written specifically for a novice clock owner who has an interest in maintaining their cuckoo clock as a hobby and does not own a shop full of expensive and sophisticated tools.

Since I started writing, this book has taken on a life of its own. As I proceed through this writing journey, I discovered that most of the clock repair skills could be broken down into simple steps that the average clock owner can understand and follow.

You probably know of or have heard about ordinary people who have started out with a hobby and become just as proficient at their passion as the trained professional, fueled by passion rather than money or creating a career.

This book assumes the reader has no prior knowledge of the subject and no specialized tools and equipment. Our journey requires minimal initial outlay.

As a member of NAWCC chapter 31 [National Association of Watch and Clock Collectors, Portland], I was persuaded to take over as an instructor of a local hands-on clock class. It turns out by teaching this class, I have learned a lot from my students. I discovered clock hobbyists are an incredible sharing group. Each member coming from a different background and experiences. Each willing to provide suggestions and tips, more of a roundtable pooling of information.

I owned many many clock books and found myself searching through several to find the answers to even the most basic student tasks. This book attempts to pool all the necessary information you need in one place.

I decided to turn this book into a class workbook aimed at the new students that walk in at the start of each term with no prior experience but a loving clock project in their arms. With each project, new questions arise. I decided to document each question/problem and their solutions in this book, so all may learn from them.

The skills I have learned on my clock journey have turned out to be useful in a surprising number of times and places in my life outside of clocks. Repairing my wife's glasses, washing machines, jewelry music box, etc, etc.

Caution, when you start working on clocks, time seems to stand still, in more ways than one. Before you know it, an hour or two has passed by as you get absorbed into your project.

About the Author

My grandfather died when I was seven. We lived in Southport, England. He had owned three grandfather clocks. About a year after he died, I asked my mother what happened to the grandfather clocks. She said they were distributed to the grandchildren. I said, "where is mine?" She said I think Auntie Florrie got one.

The next time we were visiting Auntie Florrie, I said to her, "you got my grandfather clock," in a way only an 8-year-old could without being disrespectful. I caught her off guard, but she replied, I could have it when the time was right.

As a kid, whenever I saw an old clock at a jumble sale or going cheap, I would buy it and take it apart to see how it worked. I don't think I ever got one back together again, but I enjoyed tinkering with them.

Twenty years later, when I was getting married, now living in the USA, Auntie Florrie wrote to me saying I could now have the clock.

I arranged to have the clock shipped over, and it was proudly placed in the entrance hall to my home. It was built in about 1880 in Maghull England by a local clockmaker [before the electric light was invented], had a stately mahogany case, hand-painted dial, and ran nicely.

After a few years, it stopped. I was frustrated that I didn't know what was wrong with it or how to get it going. I ended up having it serviced by a local repair shop, and it ran again. I was fascinated with the clock.

In 1995, my family decided to spend a year in England, including putting the kids in school. It was a big challenge to arrange to swap houses with an English family. Finally, we were settled, and the kids started school, my wife was volunteering at a local charity shop, and suddenly I had time on my hands.

I read the paper that morning and came across an ad for a clock course starting nearby at Manchester City College. I called the college, and they told me it was a three-year course, one day per week. I explained that I was only in the country for one year, so I persuaded them to let me take the course, coming all three days.

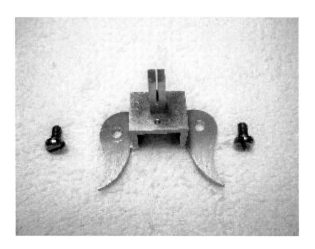

I enjoyed the course and did very well. The final exam took several weeks, making a 'suspension bridge' from scratch to exact specifications, restoring several old clocks and watches. I documented the process and took the extensive final written exam all set by BHI [British Horological Institute]. I did pass the exams and became a Horologist.

Twenty-five years later, I taught clock repair classes and 'passed it on.' This manual is the class workbook for cuckoo clocks.

SECTION ONE

Introduction

A grandfather clock, also known as a

- longcase clock
- tall-case clock
- grandfather's clock
- coffin clock
- hall clock
- standingclock
- floor clock

is a tall, freestanding, weight-driven pendulum clock with the pendulum held inside the tower or waist of the case. The case often features elaborately carved ornamentation on the hood [or bonnet], which surrounds and frames the dial or clock face.

Natives of the United Kingdom and Continental Europe by and large will still refer to what Americans call a grandfather clock as a tallcase clock or longcase clock. To put this in some historical perspective, such clocks were known the world over as longcase clocks or tallcase clocks.

The English clockmaker William Clement is credited with the development of this form in 1670. Until the early 20th century, pendulum clocks were the world's most accurate timekeeping technology, and longcase clocks, due to their superior accuracy, served as time standards for households and businesses. Today they are kept mainly for their decorative and antique value, having been widely replaced by both analog and digital timekeeping.

In 1582 sitting quietly in Pisa's cathedral, eighteen-year-old Galileo Galilei was distracted by a swinging chandelier that had been just lit by the lamplighter. His attention got caught up by its movement.

It was no surprise, being scientific-minded as he was, that Galileo began to time the swings. Having no other tools to measure, he used the steady pulse of his heartbeat. He found that no matter how wide or narrow an arc, the chandelier made, the time it took to swing from one side to the other was the same.

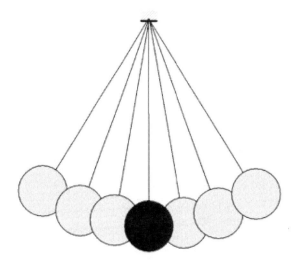

Of course, Galileo recorded his findings, but his discovery wasn't going to be just another entry in a forgotten notebook. Some years later, he experimented, trying to apply the pendulum's precise movement to the measurement of time to regulate a clock's workings. He hoped to produce a more accurate timepiece than anything before. For the rest of his life, he and his son worked at the task. But, despite his many other scientific achievements, he was ultimately unsuccessful with the clock.

In the realm of science, one discovery often leads to another, and Galileo's efforts were not in vain. For his work paved the way for Christian Huygens, a Dutch astronomer who himself was in pursuit of a more accurate clock for predicting the movement of the stars and planets.

Accuracy of time to an astronomer is like a sharp chisel to a sculptor. Precision is a must. In 1656, Huygens successfully "hitched" a pendulum to the workings of a clock. It revolutionized clock making by significantly increasing the accuracy of timepieces from fifteen minutes per day to one minute per day using a three-foot pendulum.

How did grandfather clocks get to be so tall?

A grandfather clock had to be six to nine feet tall to contain its three-foot-long pendulum, as well as its weights, which needed to drop several feet for the clock to run for any period of time.

Why is it call Grandfather clock?

There was once an American songwriter named Henry Clay Work who visited England sometime in 1875. He was staying in the George Hotel in North Yorkshire.

One day, Henry noticed quite an unusual clock sitting in the hotel's lobby, serving no real purpose. It was a large, unmoving, motionless pendulum clock with its hands completely jammed. That intrigued Henry, so he went on to inquire about its history.

The hotel's proprietors told him that the clock belonged to the late Jenkins brothers, who once owned that same hotel. The clock was intended for the older brother. It was supposedly one of the greatest and the most reliable timepieces one could ever get. However, the clock suddenly started to slow down and became less accurate when the older brother passed away. The clock is said to be 'dead' and 'silent' since then.

Although that story is more local folklore than anything, the hotel credits it as the main inspiration behind grandfather clocks.

Being a songwriter, Clay Work wrote an entire song about that whole clock incident. The song was released in 1876, and it was called "My Grandfather's Clock."

The song became popular, and fans went crazy over it. Soon enough, 'grandfather clock' became the new moniker for those longcase clocks.

Grandfather's Clock (1876)
Words and Music by Henry Clay Work

1. My grandfather's clock was too large for the shelf,
So it stood ninety years on the floor;
It was taller by half than the old man himself,
Though it weighed not a pennyweight more.
It was bought on the morn of the day that he was born,
And was always his treasure and pride;
But it stopp'd short – never to go again –
When the old man died.

CHORUS
Ninety years without slumbering [tick, tick, tick, tick],
His life seconds numbering [tick, tick, tick, tick],
It stopp'd short – never to go again –
When the old man died.

2. In watching its pendulum swing to and fro,
Many hours had he spent while a boy;
And in childhood and manhood the clock seemed to know

And to share both his grief and his joy.
For it struck twenty-four when he entered at the door,
With a blooming and beautiful bride;
But it stopp'd short – never to go again –
When the old man died.

CHORUS

3. My grandfather said that of those he could hire,
Not a servant so faithful he found;
For it wasted no time, and had but one desire –
At the close of each week to be wound.
And it kept in its place – not a frown upon its face,
And the hands never hung by its side;
But it stopp'd short – never to go again –
When the old man died.

CHORUS

4. It rang an alarm in the dead of the night –
An alarm that for years had been dumb;
And we knew that his spirit was pluming for flight –
That his hour of departure had come.
Still the clock kept the time, with a soft and muffled chime,
As we silently stood by his side;
But it stopp'd short – never to go again –
When the old man died.

CHORUS

In addition to their sentimental value when handed down through the generations, grandfather clocks are excellent timekeepers that add significant visual appeal to a home's décor. There are few pieces of furniture that are as functional, attractive, and worthy of heirloom status.

During the early years, only the nobility owned a grandfather clock. Owning one of these clocks was a sign of wealth and importance. It was not until the nineteenth century that these clocks became available to others. As the clocks became more affordable, many people began to purchase them. They are now passed down through the generations with pride.

The time it requires a pendulum to swing back and forth is figured by the pendulum's length. The pendulum's back-and-forth movement causes the weights to drop at given paces, which makes the hands move. The combined motion of the pendulum and the weights are what make a grandfather clock work, and keep such precise time.

An antique is most often defined as an object over 100 years old. This is true with grandfather clocks as well. Original glass and the decorative cut of the wood cabinet are important factors and will make an antique grandfather clock more expensive.

Types of Cases

There are four basic designs of new grandfather clock cases.

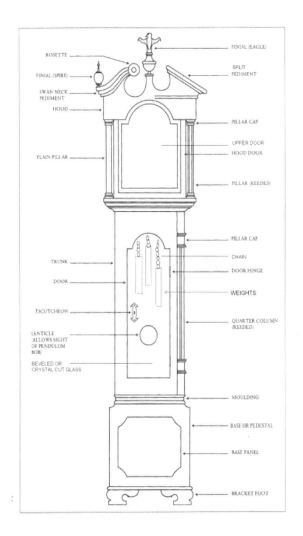

Open Pediment

Sizes

There is no official definition of the different sizes, but generally:

Grandfather is 6ft 4 inches or taller

Grandmother is 5ft 3 inches to 6ft 3 inches

Granddaughter is less than 5ft 2 inches

Arched Bonnet

Case Designs

Round Dial

English Eight Day

Flat Top

Modern Grandfather Clocks

Comtoise Clocks

These clocks were first produced during the 1680s, and their production lasted for a period of almost 230 years. Their peak production period started in 1850 and ended somewhere during 1890. During that time, about 60,000 comtoise clocks were manufactured each year. Although they were initially found only in France, their popularity eventually spread to Germany and Spain, along with a few other European regions. These clocks were later also exported further to Thailand and the Ottoman Empire.

The comtoise clock is a type of a provincial, weight-driven clock that represented, or in other words, marked the beginning of the popularizing period of clocks in France. Till the 19th century, these clocks were found wide and far across the entire country. They gained so much popularity during that period that they practically ended up ousting all other local types of clocks.

The manufacturing process of comtoise clocks was quite similar to that of Gothic clocks. They were built on huge frames that were made of iron strips. The original version of comtoise clocks was supposed to have a full, long case made with vine, but later, several variations made the clock hanging from a bracket. The long case was frequently grained and painted in the country fashion, and the sides were often tapered or were shaped like that of a violin.

Comtoise Clocks are a type of longcase clock that mainly originated in France. These clocks were specially made in the French region called Franche-Comté, which is primarily how the clock got its unique name. Since these clocks were also produced in the vicinity of Morbier in France, they were given the name 'Morbier clocks.' The name variation is simply due to the different names of areas in the Franche-Comté region.

The dials on these clocks were initially made with brass or pewter that were filled with black numerals and had a single hand. However, later, the dials were displayed on enamel cartouches, and by the 19th century, they were even made of printed paper and sometimes had a third hand that basically indicated the date.

The other versions of comtoise clocks had a pierced brass pediment that was used as a replacement for the early dials. This pediment was shaped like a rooster and had royal arms. Often times, it also had certain motifs that were basically used to represent the political enthusiasm which was alive at that point in time.

This pediment style didn't last for long, and it was replaced by other pediment styles that consisted of a variety of brass devices. The most common of these devices incorporated a pair of cornucopias in its design. Others also featured a sunburst and a basket of flowers.

Comtoise clocks faced a sudden decline in their popularity, particularly in 1871, when German clocks were allowed into the country without any taxes. This greatly affected the trade of comtoise clocks regardless of how popular they were and how diversified their output was. The First World War marked their final decline, after which the clock industry in the respective French regions was restructured for the production of more efficient and modern types of clocks.

Although a few French manufacturers were still found making these comtoise clocks toward the end of the 20th century, their initial popularity had, in fact, ultimately died down.

Bornholm Clocks

Bornholm clocks are Danish longcase clocks and were made on Bornholm from 1745 to 1900. In Sweden a unique variety of longcase clocks was made in Mora, called Mora clocks. Bornholm clock-making began in the 1740s when an English ship, which had longcase clocks in its hold, was stranded.

As the name suggests, this type of grandfather clock originated in Bornholm, which is a Danish island in the Baltic Sea. The island is situated south of Sweden, east of Denmark and north of Poland.

The production of clocks began in 1745 and lasted till 1900. These are basically Danish longcase clocks with a delicate crown, often square-shaped with a tiny window on both sides. The windows allowed one to see the working of the clock from the inside.

Interestingly, before the creation of these unique clocks, Bornholm Island had no reputation for clock-making. Its production only began when a Dutch ship that was traveling from England changed its course to the Ronne coasts. Ronne is a town on Bornholm Island, and among all other towns found on this island, Ronne is the largest of them all. Surprisingly, the ship contained five longcase or grandfather clocks in its cargo. This incident took place in 1744.

Since clocks were a rare commodity but were considered to be extremely vital back then, the sailors decided to save those clocks, and so they transported them to Paul Ottesen Arboe in Ronne. He, along with his local craftsmen, went on to repair the clocks and tried to restore the English longcase clocks. However, most of these craftsmen were turners, and they didn't really know anything about grandfather clocks.

As a result of their lack of knowledge, they had to study the mechanisms of longcase clocks before they could actually begin repairing them. So, these determined craftsmen took their time to study the clock, during which they learned all about its internal mechanisms and fully understood the structure of these longcase enclosures.

What's great about this whole learning process is that these craftsmen ended up learning so much about these clocks that they were all set to create their own version of the longcase or grandfather clock. Eventually, they did produce their own clock, which is how the Bornholm clock came into existence.

The Bornholm clock consists of lead weights, and each of them weighs almost 8 pounds. The main body of the clock is divided into three key sections: head, foot, and case. All

these sections have straight sides, but the foot often has rounded corners coupled with a four-sided molding.

The face of the clock is made of brass or iron, and it is usually adorned towards the corner, which is often made of lead. The ornamentation includes Roman numerals on tin with pierced brass hands that look absolutely beautiful. The top of the face has a little round tin placed with a five-pointed crown. This crown contains the clockmaker's name along with the year in which the clock was manufactured.

The case of the Bornholm clock, on the other hand, was usually painted with biblical motifs and sometimes had an imitation of a Chinese lakarbejde. Other variations of this clock from those times also had large bowed gesims on the case.

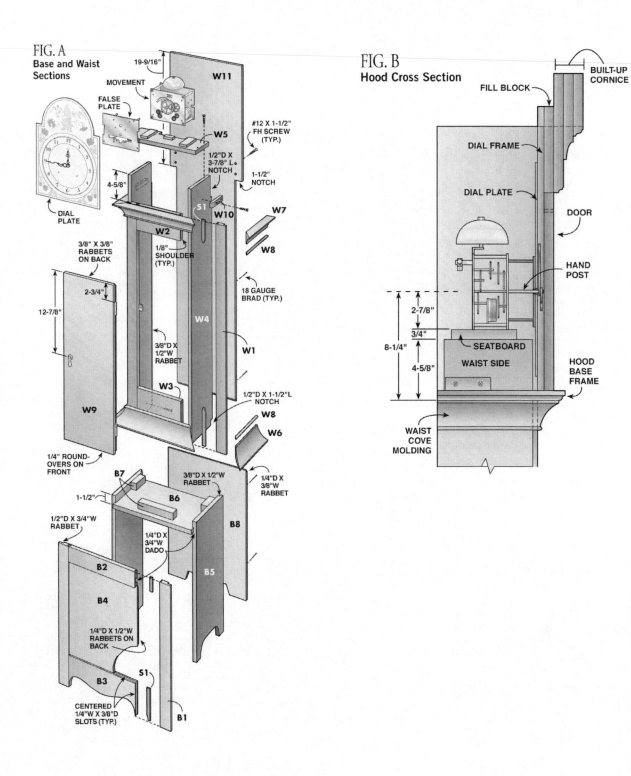

FIG. A
Base and Waist
Sections

19-9/16"

W11

MOVEMENT

FALSE
PLATE

W5

#12 X 1-1/2"
FH SCREW
(TYP.)

1/2"D X
3-7/8" L
NOTCH

1-1/2"
NOTCH

4-5/8"

S1

W10

W7

DIAL
PLATE

W2

W8

3/8" X 3/8"
RABBETS
ON BACK

1/8"
SHOULDER
(TYP.)

2-3/4"

18 GAUGE
BRAD (TYP.)

12-7/8"

W4

3/8"D X
1/2"W
RABBET

W1

W3

1/2"D X 1-1/2"L
NOTCH

W8

W9

W6

1/4" ROUND-
OVERS ON
FRONT

B7

3/8"D X 1/2"W
RABBET

1/4"D X
3/8"W
RABBET

1-1/2"

B6

B8

1/2"D X 3/4"W
RABBET

1/4"D X
3/4"W
DADO

B2

B5

B4

1/4"D X 1/2"W
RABBETS ON
BACK

B3

S1

CENTERED
1/4"W X 3/8"D
SLOTS (TYP.)

B1

FIG. B
Hood Cross Section

FILL BLOCK

BUILT-UP
CORNICE

DIAL FRAME

DIAL PLATE

DOOR

HAND
POST

2-7/8"

3/4"

8-1/4"

SEATBOARD

WAIST SIDE

HOOD
BASE
FRAME

4-5/8"

WAIST
COVE
MOLDING

Lateral view of a longcase clock movement without a striking mechanism, the mid-1800s.

The advent of the longcase clock is due to the invention of the anchor escapement mechanism by Robert Hooke around 1658. Prior to the adoption of the anchor mechanism, pendulum clock movements used an older verge escapement mechanism, which required very wide pendulum swings of about 80–100°.

Long pendulums with such wide swings could not be fitted within a case, so most freestanding clocks had short pendulums.

Lateral view of a Timothy Mason longcase clock movement with striking mechanism, circa 1730

The anchor mechanism reduced the pendulum's swing to around 4° to 6°, allowing clockmakers to use longer pendulums, which had slower "beats." These consumed less power allowing clocks to run longer between windings, caused less friction and wear in the movement, and were more accurate. Almost all longcase clocks use a seconds pendulum [also called a "Royal" pendulum] meaning that each swing [or half-period] takes one second. These are about 39 inches long [to the center of the bob), requiring a long narrow case.

The long narrow case actually predated the anchor clock by a few decades, appearing in clocks in 1660 to allow a long drop for the powering weights. However, once the second's pendulum began to be used, this long weight case proved perfect to house it as well.

British clockmaker William Clement, who disputed credit for the anchor escapement with Robert Hooke, made the first longcase clocks by 1680. Later the same year, Thomas Tompion, the most prominent British clockmaker, was making them too. Longcase clocks spread rapidly from England to other European countries and Asia.

The first longcase clocks, like all clocks prior to the anchor escapement, had only one hand; an hour hand. The increased accuracy made possible by the anchor motivated the addition of the minute hand to clock faces in the next few decades.

Between 1680 and 1800, the average price of a grandfather clock in England remained steady at £1 10s. In 1680, this was the amount paid by an average working family for a year's rent, so the purchase of clocks was confined to the relatively well-off. But by 1800, wages had increased enough so that many lower middle-class households owned grandfather clocks.

Modern longcase clocks use a more accurate variation of the anchor escapement called the deadbeat escapement.

One-Day Movement

This is also called the 30-hour movement, and its key requirement is winding daily. Longcase clocks that run on a one-day movement only have a single weight. It is supposed to use that weight for two purposes: to run the striking mechanism and to drive the timekeeping system.

This style of movement was considered to be largely inexpensive and was also meant for those people who couldn't afford to buy eight-day movement clocks.

Eight-Day Movement

This movement style requires you to wind it only once a week, and unlike the one-day movement, this style is run with the help of two weights. One weight drives the striking mechanism while the other propels the pendulum. The striking mechanism of this movement basically consists of a bell or chime. It also has two keyholes on either side of the dial that are used during the winding process.

The movement typically sits on a seatboard which is secured to the movement with seatboard hooks. The seatboard sits on the wider wood case.

Striking and Chiming

In the early 20th century, quarter-hour chime sequences were added to longcase clocks. At the top of each hour, the full chime sequence sounds, immediately followed by the hour strike. At 15 minutes after each hour, 1/4 of the chime sequence plays, at the bottom of each hour, 1/2 of the chime sequence plays, and at 15 minutes before each hour, 3/4 of the chime sequence plays.

The chime tune used in almost all longcase clocks is Westminster Quarters. Many also offer the option of Whittington chimes or St. Michael's chimes, selectable by a switch mounted on the right side of the dial, which also allows one to silence the chimes if desired.

As a result of adding chime sequences, all modern mechanical longcase clocks have three weights instead of just two. The left weight provides power for the hour strike, the middle weight provides power for the clock's pendulum and general timekeeping functions, while the right weight provides power for the quarter-hour chime sequences.

A striking clock is a clock that sounds the hours audibly on a bell or gong. In 12-hour striking, used most commonly in striking clocks today, the clock strikes once at 1:00 A.M., twice at 2:00 A.M., continuing in this way up to twelve times at 12:00 P.M., then starts again, striking once at 1:00 P.M., twice at 2:00 P.M., up to twelve times at 12:00 A.M.

The striking feature of clocks was originally more important than their clock faces; the earliest clocks struck the hours, but had no dials to enable the time to be read. The development of mechanical clocks in 12th century Europe was motivated by the need to ring bells upon the canonical hours to call the community to prayer. The earliest known mechanical clocks were large striking clocks installed in towers in monasteries or public squares, so that their bells could be heard far away. Though an early striking clock in Syria was a 12-hour clock, many early clocks struck up to 24 strokes, particularly in Italy, where the 24-hour clock, keeping Italian hours, was widely used in the 14th and 15th centuries.

As the modern 12-hour clock became more widespread, particularly in Great Britain and Northern Europe, 12-hour striking became more widespread and eventually became the standard. In addition to striking on the hour, many striking clocks play sequences of chimes on the quarter-hours. The most common sequence is Westminster Quarters.

Today the time-disseminating function of clock striking is almost no longer needed, and striking clocks are kept for historical, traditional, and aesthetic reasons. Historic clock towers in towns, universities, and religious institutions worldwide still strike the hours, famous examples being Big Ben in London, the Peace Tower in Ottawa, and the Kremlin Clock in Moscow. Home striking in grandfather clocks is very common.

A typical striking clock will have two gear trains, because a striking clock must add a striking train that operates the mechanism that rings the bell in addition to the timekeeping train that measures the passage of time.

English 8-day bell strike

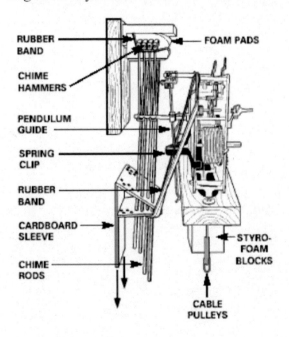

RUBBER BAND — FOAM PADS
CHIME HAMMERS
PENDULUM GUIDE
SPRING CLIP
RUBBER BAND
CARDBOARD SLEEVE
CHIME RODS
STYRO-FOAM BLOCKS
CABLE PULLEYS

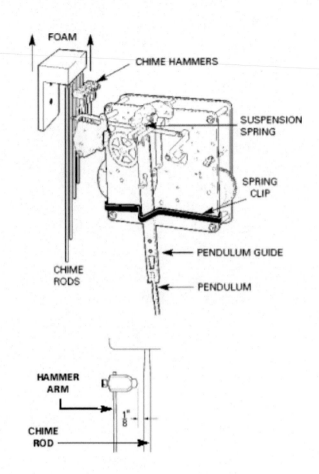

FOAM
CHIME HAMMERS
SUSPENSION SPRING
SPRING CLIP
CHIME RODS
PENDULUM GUIDE
PENDULUM

HAMMER ARM
CHIME ROD

Movement with chime rods

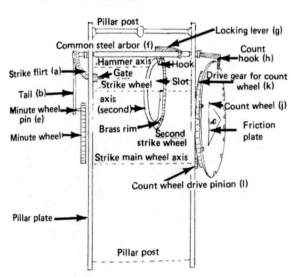

Pillar post
Common steel arbor (f)
Locking lever (g)
Count hook (h)
Strike flirt (a)
Hammer axis
Hook
Gate
Drive gear for count wheel (k)
Strike wheel
Slot
Tail (b)
Strike wheel axis (second)
Count wheel (j)
Minute wheel pin (e)
Brass rim
Friction plate
Minute wheel
Second strike wheel
Strike main wheel axis
Count wheel drive pinion (l)
Pillar plate
Pillar post

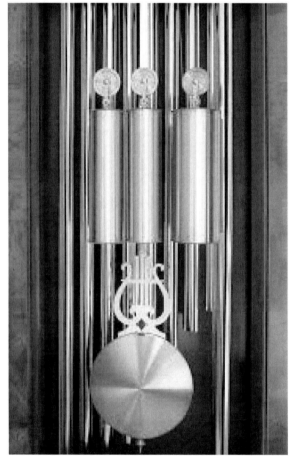

Movement with tubular bells

Movement with bells

The clock's face is known as its "dial" and can be made of polished brass, pained or enameled metal.

The numbers can be Arabic or Roman. It is expected that the numeral for the number four use four battons rather than the usual VI as this looks more balanced against the eight on the other side of the dial.

By 1730, enamel dials were sometimes produced in the 1780s for longcase clocks, but are very rare. More common are painted enamel dials, fitted to high-quality pieces.

Enamel sections are most frequently found on French clocks. Often the dials are gilt, with the numerals set against enamel reserves. Enamel dials are incredibly prone to cracking and chipping, so examine examples very carefully. Hairline cracks are often camouflaged by bleaching, but you should be able to spot the color differences. Cracking crates a cobweb effect over the dial.

Wooden painted dials were used for tavern clocks in England from the mid - 18th century. They are usually 12 inch square, with an arch above, painted white, and then decorated with flowers before being varnished. Wooden dials are susceptible to woodworm and are often in split condition. They can be appropriately restored by specialists.

The brass dials you see on longcase clocks were probably once silvered, but the silvering has been polished away over the years. The effect is achieved by using silvering salts, which change the color of the brass. Re-silvering is not expensive but should be done by a specialist. Like re-gilding, this kind of restoration is regarded as sympathetic.

Early clocks had elementary, finely sculpted blued-steel hands [whereby the steel was polished and blued with a flame, preventing the metal from rusting and giving a distinctly burnished blue appearance] in straight-forward designs. Along with the style of dials, the hands became more elaborate. Blued steel gave way to gilt metal in the latter half of the 18th century on country longcase clocks. Hands get damaged and are often repaired, but it only affects value significantly if the clock is a top-quality one, and the replacements are very obvious.

With older European long case clocks, the movement is typically made by one person or company and the dial by another, so an additional item is added called a falseplate made of castiron, that allows any dial to be fitted to any movement, with the connection happening at the falseplate. Basically, a mounting plate.

The falseplate is connected to the movement and then the dial is connected to the falseplate using dial feet and taper pins.

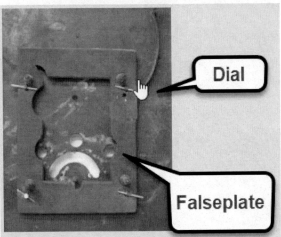

Dial

Falseplate

Falseplate

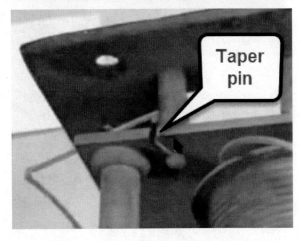

Taper pin

There is usually a maker name on the falseplate that can help date the clock. A piece of chalk rubbed over the name will reveal the name better.

As clocks became more affordable to the public in the mid-1700s, competition encouraged adding more complexity to clocks. Local clockmakers purchased standard movements and adapted them to the local customer's needs.

At that time, there were no streetlights so knowing the phases of the moon was helpful. Farmers also needed to know the phases of the moon for crop planting, based on local knowledge of the moon's influences.

Each clockmaker seems to have their own way of incorporating moon mechanisms into the clocks they had for sale which is the reason there are so many different methods and parts used.

As the clocks became older and needed servicing, it was often the moon mechanism that caused the clock to malfunction. The moon phases being less important by then, the extra parts were simply removed by the owner or clockmaker and the working clock returned to service. So, it is now very common to find moon dial clocks with missing parts.

Modern clock owners and collectors now want to restore clocks back to the original operating condition.

My experience and research have revealed dozens of moon dial designs but here I will focus on five that demonstrate the concept of the mechanism so new parts can be created and fitted.

Start by studying the existing front of the movement, falseplate, and back of the dial to identify where the missing parts likely were located. Look for posts that no longer have a function, bent or missing pins. Study the following examples and create parts, first from wood to make the moon dial operate again and finetune the design before fabricating more durable metal parts. The moon dial should make one full rotation every 29 ½ days. A typical moon dial will have 118 teeth, so it needs a tooth to be given a push every 12 hours. The moon dial needs to advance two teeth each day which is easily achieved by synchronizing it with the hour wheel or snail. A click spring ensures only one tooth is advanced for each push.

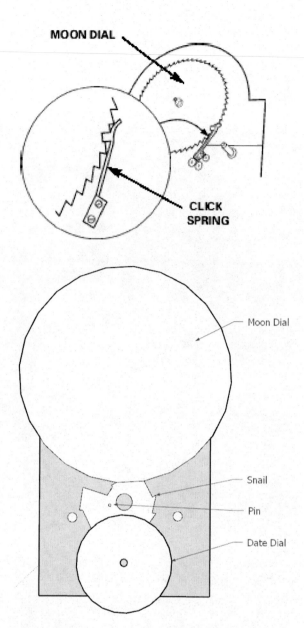

Rear of the Dial

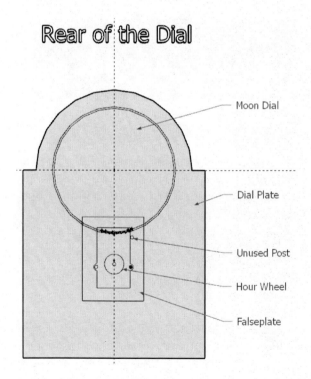

Typical Rear of the Dial with moon dial. Note the unused post.

This first example is the simplest. A pin on the snail advances one moon dial tooth each time the hour wheel rotates. This pin might be bent, broken off or have been removed. This repair is as simple as straightening or replacing the pin.

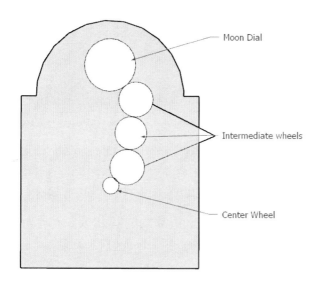

This movement has a very small moon dial and requires three intermediate wheels each of 48 teeth to transfer the hour wheel movement to the moon dial.

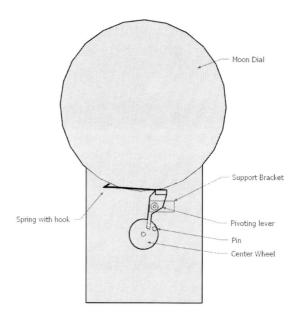

This simple design uses a spring with a hook on it, operated by the pin on the snail moving the pivot lever twice per day.

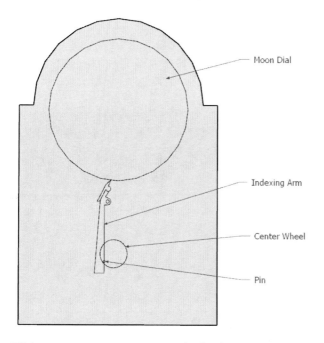

This movement uses an indexing arm to advance the moon dial operated from a pin on the center wheel. The head of the indexing arm pivots on the backstroke, so the moon dial does not move back again.

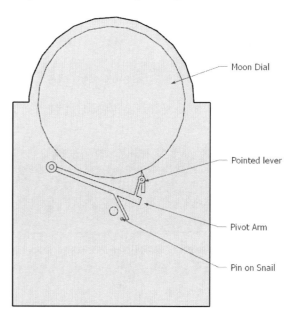

With this system, the pin on the snail lifts the Pivot Arm which engages the Pointed Lever in a tooth on the Moon Dial. The moon dial will be advanced two teeth per day.

Setting up a Grandfather clock

This description assumes you have just purchased a new or used grandfather clock, or have moved to a new location.

Unpack your Grandfather Clock

Level Your Grandfather Clock

You clock must be level, plumb and secured to the wall.

It is best not to place the clock on an outside wall or near an external door or window that will be left open.

Extra care will be needed if it is to set on carpet. Typically, when the carpet is installed, a tack strip is placed next to the wall. This will have the effect of tipping the clock away from the wall. In this case, place the clock on a nice piece of hardwaood, positioned away from the tack strip.

Once you are sure the clock is level and plumb, secure the clock to the wall, into a stud,m or using sturdy toggle bolts. This will ensure the clock will not move if bumped or subjected to earthquake movement.

Unpacking your chimes and install in the clock [if the clock has chime rods or tubular bells]

Install the movement into the clock, making sure the seatboard is level both sideways and front to back. Make sure the chime hammers lign up with the chime bars or tubular bells.

Feed the chain or cable through the seat board and prepare for the installation of the weights.

Hang the Pendulum Hook the pendulum on the suspension spring

Hang each weight on its weight pulley. Assuming the weights are correctly marked, make sure they are installed on the correct pully [facing the clock, left, center and right]

Set the Time. Move ONLY the minute hand clockwise until the correct time is set. Do NOT move the hour hand to set the time.

Start the Clock. Pull the pendulum to the far left and release to start the swing.

Regulate the Time by adjusting the regulating nut at the bottom of the pendumlum. If the clock runs too slow [loses time each day], turn the adjustment nut to the right. If the clock runs too fast [gains time each day], turn the adjustment nut to the left.

Note: One complete turn equals approximately 1/2 minute per day.

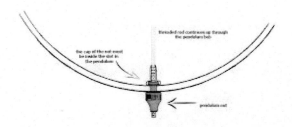

back view of adjustable pendulum

Winding a Crank-Wound Clock

Look for the winding points. If your grandfather clock is wound by a crank or a key, it should have one to three small holes on the clock face. Most commonly, these are located near the 3 (III), the 9 (IX), the center, or anywhere in the lower half of the clock face. If you do not see a hole, and your clock did not come with a crank or key, see the instructions for chain-wound clocks instead.

Obtain a clock crank or key of the correct size. Newly purchased clocks of this type should come with a key or crank, but if you acquired a used clock, or misplaced the winding implement, you can find a new one online or from a clockmaker. Open the door protecting the clock face, and measure the width of each hole precisely using a ruler or tape measure with a millimeter scale (mm), or preferably a set of calipers that can measure in 0.25 mm increments. Purchase a crank or key with this shaft width for safe and easy winding. You may wish to purchase three or four winding implements in different sizes, in case your measurement was slightly off.

Note: When purchasing a crank, make sure the length of the shaft is sufficient to raise the crank above the level of the clock hands, so you can turn it 360° without damaging them.

Some manufacturers sell keys in a numbered scale, rather than by shaft width. However, there is no single industry-wide scale, so referring to the exact millimeter size is recommended.

Use the crank or key to wind the first weight. Gently push the shaft of the crank or key into any one of the winding holes. It should be a snug fit, but do not force it in. Gently hold the clock face steady with one hand and use the other to gently turn the crank. Try turning in both directions, and see which one moves smoothly; each individual clock winds either clockwise or counterclockwise. One of the long weights lower down in the clock should rise as you turn. Stop turning right before the weight touches the wooden "seat board," or when the key no longer easily turns.

If you cannot turn the key easily, or you do not see a weight moving, check to see if one of the weights is already at the top. If one or more of the chimes is turned off, the weight responsible for timing that chime will not fall, and does not need to be wound.

The weights are typically located above the pendulum. You may or may not need to open the lowercase in order to see them.

Repeat the process for the other winding points. If your clock has more than one weight, it should also have more than one winding point in the clock face. Move the crank or key to the remaining winding points, turning it in each one until every weight is nearly touching the wooden board above it.

If necessary, make adjustments carefully. Now is a good time to check whether the clock is still displaying the correct time. If not, you may physically move only the minute hand to the correct time, moving it clockwise only. Always stop at the 12 (XII) and allow the clock to strike the hour before continuing. Do the same for other points if the clock chimes at additional times [typically the quarter hours at the 3, 6, and 9].

There are some clocks that can safely have their minute hand turned counterclockwise, but do not risk it unless you are certain. If the minute hand "resists" attempts to move it clockwise, and can move smoothly counterclockwise, you may have an unusual model that should be adjusted counterclockwise.

If your clock is running too fast or too slow, find the knob or nut at the bottom of the swinging pendulum. Tighten it clockwise in order to slow the clock down, or loosen it counterclockwise to speed it up.

Wind weekly, or as necessary. Almost all grandfather clocks are made to run for seven or eight days without winding, so winding them on the same day each week will ensure that it never stops. If your clock stops before its regular winding time, however, you may need to wind it more frequently.

Winding a Chain-Wound Clock

Look for chains hanging next to the weights. Open the door protecting the long, hanging weights in the clock case (not the pendulum). Most clocks have one, two, or three weights, but there may be more on unusual models. If you see a hanging chain next to each weight, your clock is probably chain-wound.

If you cannot find either a chain or a winding hole in the clock face, ask someone to help you look, or consult a professional clockmaker or clock repair shop.

Gently pull on one of the chains. Grasp a chain hanging next to a weight that is not at the top of the case. Slowly pull down on the chain and watch the weight rise. Continue until the weight is almost touching the board at the top of the weight case, or until you cannot move the weight by pulling at the same gentle rate.

Pull on the chain next to a weight, never the chain the weight is attached to.

It does not matter which weight you wind first.

Repeat with the other weights. Each weight has its own chain. Gently pull on each of these until the weight associated with it has nearly touched the board above the weights. Your clock is fully wound once all the weights are in the top-most position.

Typically, the center weight controls the clock's timekeeping. If other weights are present, they control the hour strike, or the quarter-hour chime.

Make adjustments if necessary. Physically rotate the minute hand, not the hour hand, of the clock if you need to set the time. Rotate clockwise unless you feel resistance in that direction, and use your free hand to steady the clock face as you turn. Be gentle to avoid bending or breaking the clock hand, and stop and wait for the clock to strike or time before continuing to move the hand.

1. REMOVE THE WEIGHTS FROM THE CLOCK

The first thing to do when getting a Grandfather Clock ready to move is remove the weights and pendulum from inside the clock. If the weights were left on, they could swing around during transport and potentially shatter the glass surrounding them.

Insert several folded pieces of packing paper above each pulley holding the cables. Wind up the weights all the way to the top, one at a time, until the paper pieces get pressed against each pulley. This safety step guarantees that the cables will remain taut when the weights are removed.

If you own a chain-driven grandfather clock, then you'll need to make sure its chains do not get damaged or broken during the house move. Use your hands to stop the pendulum from swinging. Wind up the weights halfway, about three-quarters of the entire length. DO NOT pull the weights all the way up because that can damage the chains and their sprockets. Insert cable ties just below the sprocket of each set of chains, then fix those ties in place. This step will guarantee that the clock chains won't fall off their sprockets during transport.

Using soft cotton gloves, gently unhook each clock weight and see on its bottom whether it's been pre-labeled. If it is marked, then that's good – you'll only need to pack it properly. If it's not marked, then you're going to have to label each weight Left, center and right.

2. WRAP THE WEIGHTS AND PENDULUM IN A MOVING BLANKET TO PROTECT THEM FROM DAMAGE

The weights will be wrapped individually in think blankets to avoid being scratched during the move. Great care should be taken with each piece of the clock to keep everything exactly as it was.

DISASSEMBLE: Protect the chime rods.

Do your best to protect every single component of your grandfather clock.

Some grandfather clock models come with chime rods, and if your long-case clock does too, then you'll also need to protect those rods during the haul.

The thing to remember here is that chime rods are pretty fragile and may break if they are left without any sort of protection. The worst part is that most chime rods are extremely difficult to replace, so whatever you do, don't skip this step.

To protect the chime rods when moving, position small pieces of bubble wrap between the rods, then use tape to fix the protective material. This way, the metal rods cannot get into contact with one another and won't get accidentally damaged.

DISASSEMBLE: Remove glass shelves and wooden ornaments

To transport a grandfather clock safely, you'll have to remove any glass shelves it may have. Do this very carefully as you don't want to drop any of the glass components of your pendulum clock, and you don't want to cut yourself on the glass either.

Also, take off any decorative wooden ornaments that

- can be removed safely, and
- look too fragile to survive the move unscathed.

Pack both glass elements and wood ornaments in packing paper first, then in protective moving blankets.

Finally, re-install the side access panel of your grandfather clock and lock it in position. That access panel [or panels] has to be there so that the glass windows of the long-case clock won't come out.

3. PLACE MOVING BLANKETS INSIDE THE CLOCK TO STABILIZE GLASS FROM THE INSIDE

Inside the grandfather clock, two of our thick blankets should be placed inside. The blankets are to help stabilize the glass from the inside to keep it from breaking. Take extra care to make sure that the blankets on the inside are not stuffed in carelessly or too tight. The glass on a grandfather clock is so fragile that even blankets stuffed in too tight could shatter the glass from the inside.

At this point take the opportunity to secure the key to the door of the clock at the top.

4. WRAP THE OUTSIDE OF THE CLOCK TO PROTECT IT FROM DAMAGE

Now that the inside is secure, we are ready to get the outside ready to be moved. Don't leave any sections unprotected and use as many blankets as you need to provide a good level of protection for your valuable possession.

Use packing tape to secure the blankets but be careful not to touch the clock surface directly with the tape because doing so will most likely damage the delicate finish.

The final product is a grandfather clock adequately packed up and ready to be moved to its next destination.

Have several people to help with the move and use a suitable furniture dolly.

MOVE: Keep your grandfather clock upright

Exercise extreme caution while you're wheeling your grandfather clock out of your home. Be sure to go slowly and to never rush things, even when time is against you.

You must do your best to keep your grandfather clock upright at all times. Laying down the clock during transport is not recommended as it may damage the finely-tuned clockwork mechanism inside it.

Antique furniture clocks are even more susceptible to transportation damage when they are laid down on their sides or on their back because of the way their movements are fixed to the case.

Once safely inside the moving vehicle, strap well the grandfather clock to the side to restrict any unwanted movement during the relocation trip.

For hobbyists and do-it-yourself owners, pendulum clocks present the advantage of being serviceable. The components of a pendulum clock are usually visible and replaceable, when suitable parts can be found, allowing a clock owner to repair a pendulum clock as its components break down. This is very different from an electronic clock that features circuitry and a sealed case that prevents tampering and repair.

Another advantage of grandfather clocks is the movement and its components are much larger than most other types of clocks, making their repair and maintenance much easier for the novice clock owner.

Chimes out of Sequence

A grandfather clock with a Westminster tune, if working correctly, will play the following notes in this sequence:

At ¼ past each hour, you will hear four notes.

At ½ past each hour, you will typically hear eight notes

At ¾ past the hour, you will typically hear 12 notes

On the hour [before hearing the number of hours chimed], you will typically hear 16 notes.

Many times the chiming will get out of sequence due to many reasons. If you have just adjusted the time and the chiming is out of sequence, just allow the clock to catch up to itself. By allowing the clock to run for an hour or 2, the grandfather clock will catch up to itself, and the chiming will be back into sequence.

If you have allowed the Grandfather clock to run for a few hours and it did not catch up to itself, then the minute hand is in the wrong position. Follow the following steps to correct this:

- Move the minute hand 15 minutes at a time until the grandfather clock chimes the hour. Then stop. Do not be concerned about where the minute hand is pointing at this time.
- Leaving the minute hand in this position, unscrew the nut that holds the hands in place.
- Remove the minute hand.
- Reposition the minute hand so that it is pointing to the hour.
- Reinstall the nut that holds the minute hand in place.

The minute hand has a square hole on the base that allows you to position the hand on a square shaft. The minute hand can be installed in one of four positions; however, only one place is correct.

Hour Strikes Out Of Sequence

If your grandfather clock strikes the wrong hour, this is usually a quick fix and will only take a moment to repair.

The HOUR HAND ONLY can be moved forwards or backward without any problem. If the clock is striking the wrong hour, you can simply rotate the HOUR HAND in either direction to the correct hour the clock is chiming. Here is an example. Keep in mind your hour or hand position may be different.

EXAMPLE: The grandfather clock is striking 12 times; however, the clock is indicating 9 O'clock.

- 1 After the grandfather clock stops chiming 12, gently grasp the HOUR HAND only and move it either way to the position of 12. Use caution here and make sure you do not move the minute hand or bend either the HOUR HAND or the minute hand.

- 2 Using your fingernails on your thumb, gently press the HOUR HAND downward slightly. Be careful and do not press so hard that the HOUR HAND touches the face of the clock.

- 3 The grandfather clock hour strike should now be back in sequence.

Securing a Longcase Clock

Longcase clocks are almost always top-heavy and should be secured to the wall. Screw an eyelet screw [medium size screw with a circle on the end] to the wall and top of the clock, then connect the two with a wire. Well worth a hole in the wall and the clock to keep the kids safe.

SEE PART TWO OF THIS BOOK FOR DETAILED INSTRUCTIONS ON HOW CLOCKS WORK AND HOW TO REPAIR THEM.

Brass Dials

If your grandfather clock has a brass dial, it was probably made in the period between 1680 and 1770, and most likely between 1700 and 1770. The ones made before 1700 are very rare. Most of them only had one hand because the average person had no need to know the time to the nearest minute, and with a bit of experience, you can tell the time to the nearest five minutes on one of these early clocks.

By 1730 the vast majority of grandfather clocks had two hands for the hours and minutes. One-handed clocks continued to be made in country areas for a long time, so one hand is not a guarantee of an early clock but is a good guide. Village life was very conservative, and the people living in villages at this time still had no real need for "to the minute" time.

From around 1730 -1770 (all these figures are approximate) the brass dial clock was made all over England in ever-increasing numbers, and the dials became more ornate as time went on, especially on the eight-day clocks. More features appeared, such as seconds hands in a small subsidiary dial, date hands or wheels, and moon phases, usually in an arch on top of the dial, but sometimes in a small aperture in the dial itself.

Here are a few more features to look for when dating your clock: -

Brass dials continued to be made in the Southern counties until 1830 or even later.

The later Southern clocks usually have a dial, which is a single sheet of thin brass, silvered all over and resembling an early painted dial at first glance. Period 1800 onwards.

Another late feature on Southern dials was a plain, un-matted engraved and silvered dial center - C.1775 onwards.

Brass dials tended to simplify again from C.1750 onwards. The decorative half-hour markers were replaced by an easier to engrave simple diamond shape or left off altogether.

Dial centers were matted till C.1700, then engraved all over with foliage type designs till C.1730. Some dials were then engraved over a matted center, the Sam Lomax dial below right is a good example of this. Eventually, most clocks went back to a plain or matted center again. Yes, it can all get a bit confusing at times - - -

Early 8 day dials had decorative rings around the winding holes, these were left off from C.1750 onwards.

The lunette date aperture appeared C. 1750, with a fixed hand pointing to the date number. (see Lomax dial below) The date numbers were engraved on a wheel that revolved behind the dial to show the current date number.

From C.1760 onwards, the edges of any cut-outs on the dial were scalloped for decoration, moon phase, seconds, date, etc. This feature started to appear in C1760 and continued afterward on good quality work.

Early clocks 1680 to 1700 had a small dial, eight or nine inches square. 1700 to 1740, the size went to ten inches square, 1740 to 1770, the dial is likely to be eleven inches, and by 1770 the size went to twelve inches and stayed that size. There are exceptions to these sizes, but they are a good general guide when taken with other features.

Another date clue I have noticed during clock repairs is that any screws in an early movement (1680 to 1750) have square heads. After 1750 the screw heads are round, and the thread profile is a better cut.

From 1730 longcase clocks ceased being made in London. The clockmakers followed the demands of fashion and made bracket or shelf clocks. Provincial clockmakers, many trained in London, made large numbers of longcase clocks from 1700 right through to 1880, when imports of cheap German and American wall and mantle clocks put an end to the making of longcase clocks altogether.

A "bird-cage" movement (it has vertical pillars, and the plates are horizontal top and bottom) is often taken to be a sign of an early clock. This is not guaranteed; however, in Southern England, the clockmakers continued to make this type of movement from the start right through to 1820. The bird-cage movement is a guide to location, not date. Very few Northern makers used this movement. It was essentially the same as the even earlier Lantern Clock movement. Northern makers had no tradition of making these clocks, so used the normal plated movement (vertical plates, horizontal pillars) from the start of their clockmaking.

Some case features - - - Early clock trunk doors fit flush inside the door opening. From 1730 onwards, the door was given a larger edge and covered the hole sides by fitting against the case front.

A convex molding under the hood is another reliable sign of a pre-1710 clock. After this date again, with a very few exceptions, usually in rural areas, the moldings were always concave.

Hood pillars were barley-sugar twist until 1705, then either plain or fluted after this date. Up to C. 1700, the hood pillars were attached to the hood door and opened with it. Some Southern clocks continued this to the end of the brass dial period. Still, by 1715 the vast majority were separate from the door, fitted to the hood frame.

Cast brass capitals were fitted to the columns on the hood and on the trunk if fitted, from 1740 onwards on the more expensive clocks.

Country clocks often have a rather plain, but nicely proportioned Oak case, often with a flat top, but after 1740 the fashion came in to put horns on the top, often decorated with round wood or brass facings.

The "caddy" top was used from 1690 to 1710, then the fashion changed to the "pagoda" top, often with three ball and spire decorations screwed on the right, left and center. This type of hood top carried on from 1740 right to the end of the brass dial period.

Marquetry was used on top-end cases in London from 1675 to 1720. There are almost no provincial marquetry cases.

Japanned or Lacquered cases were fashionable from 1725 to 1770. Some Northern examples are around, but many were stripped back to the wood years ago when our climate caused the finish to deteriorate badly.

Pendulums too, have a time progression, 1680 to 1740. They had a thin wire rod with a small rounded bob, often plain lead. From 1740 to 1800, the wire rod stayed, but the bob became flattened into a saucer shape, around four inches in diameter, often with a brass case. The late ones 1800 to 1880 have a wide flat strip of iron instead of the wire rod and the same four-inch brass-faced bob. Sometimes the bob is cast iron with a decorative pattern and painted gold or black.

Lead weights were always used until C. 1770. Quality clocks had brass-cased lead weights. Cast Iron weights were used on nearly all painted dial clocks - - - a cast-iron weight on a brass dial clock is not original.

A good reliable sign of an early clock is the half-hour marker (between the big roman numerals) being a cross with arrowheads. The base of the cross runs right down into the chapter ring edge. C. 1670 to 1705.

The same early clocks had the minutes numbered inside the minute band, and quite small C. 1670 to 1695. From 1695 the minute ring is moved inwards on the chapter ring, and the numbers engraved outside the minute ring.

Another clue - - - the minute number 5 had a short tail until 1710, this tail grew longer over time, by 1750 the tail almost curled right round to form a circle. Easier to see than describe, but unmistakable once you have seen it.

A bit of detective work looking for all the clues, then taking them all together should enable you to have a very good idea of when your clock was made. If the dial has a signature and place name, this is another helpful source of information. There are several directories of clockmakers available - - - don't be too disappointed if your clockmaker is not listed. There were many, many one-man makers working in England who only made a few clocks altogether because they were busy farming, or weaving, or blacksmithing and made the clocks in winter for an extra income.

South in these notes means all the South of England, as far up as the South Midlands. North means Birmingham to Scotland.

If you are thinking of buying a clock, these notes should help you to avoid some of the "altered" clocks, of which there are many - - - unscrupulous antique dealers used to put a good brass dial eight-day movement in a nice Mahogany case to increase it's value. (This is called a "marriage" by the dealers) Of course, they then put the painted dial movement in the plain Oak or Pine case and sold it off cheaply. Unfortunately, there are lots of these clocks around still, if you want a nice original clock, you need to know what to look for.

An early 10" brass dial, one-handed, circa 1710

A later 12" brass dial, circa 1760

CLUES TO THE DATE CAN BE FOUND IN THE HANDS, MOVEMENT PILLARS, AND SPANDRELS. THESE FEATURES ARE NOT ABSOLUTE, BUT BY TAKING THEM TOGETHER WITH OTHER INDICATORS A GOOD IDEA OF THE DATE TO WITHIN TEN YEARS CAN BE FOUND.

Hands

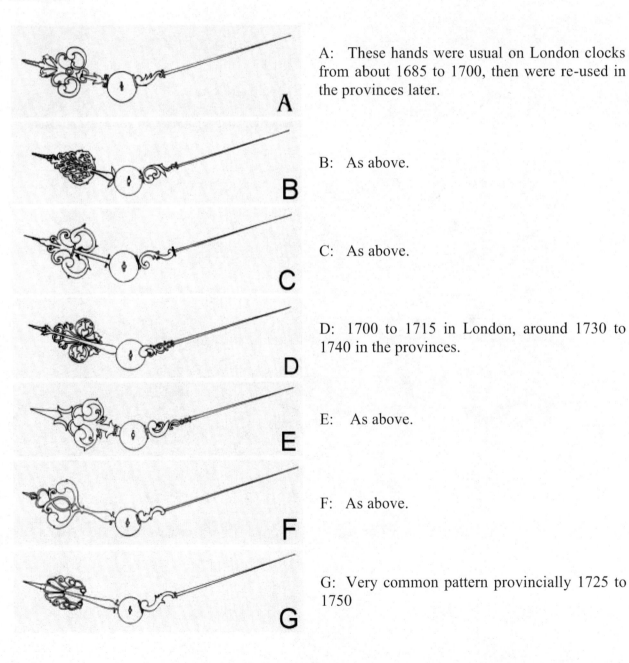

A: These hands were usual on London clocks from about 1685 to 1700, then were re-used in the provinces later.

B: As above.

C: As above.

D: 1700 to 1715 in London, around 1730 to 1740 in the provinces.

E: As above.

F: As above.

G: Very common pattern provincially 1725 to 1750

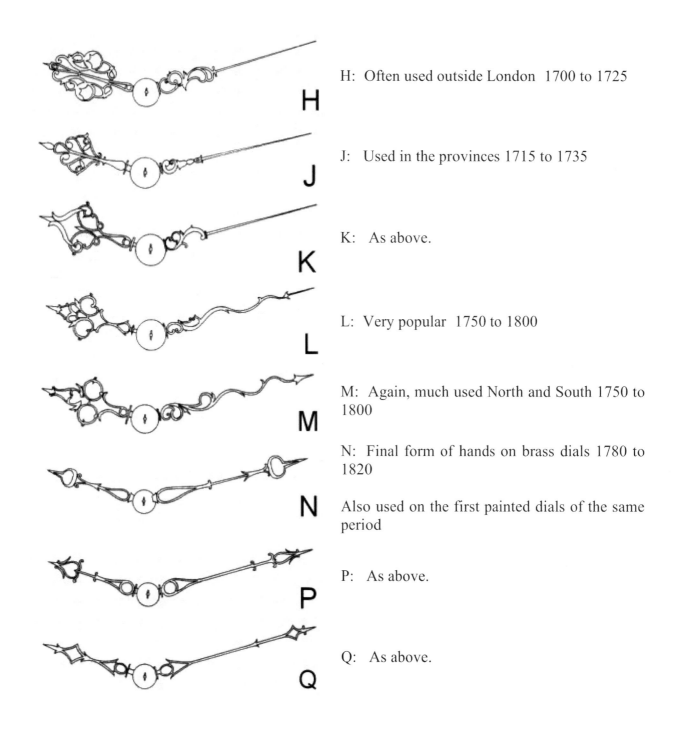

H: Often used outside London 1700 to 1725

J: Used in the provinces 1715 to 1735

K: As above.

L: Very popular 1750 to 1800

M: Again, much used North and South 1750 to 1800

N: Final form of hands on brass dials 1780 to 1820

Also used on the first painted dials of the same period

P: As above.

Q: As above.

Movement Pillars

No 1 An early period "finned" pillar, often used by London makers, and good provincial clockmakers. 1660 to 1740

No 2 middle period, very common pattern 1740 to 1800

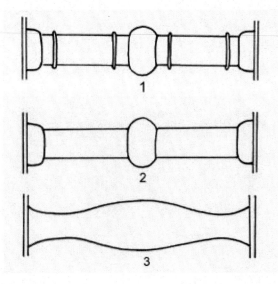

No 3 Late period pattern, 1800 and after.

Dial Spandrels

[These tend to be a better date guide than hands, which were often broken and replaced]

1. London, pre 1700, very rare on provincial clocks

2. First appeared C1685, peak use provinces

1695 to 1710

3. Often used by Thomas Thompion, but appears

1695 to 1730 on provincial clocks.

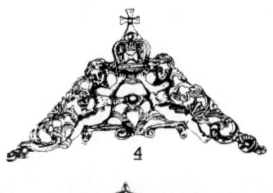

4. Very popular outside London 1700 to 1725

Can be seen on the early brass dial pictured above.

5. A large spandrel, mainly used in Northern England

C 1750 to 1775

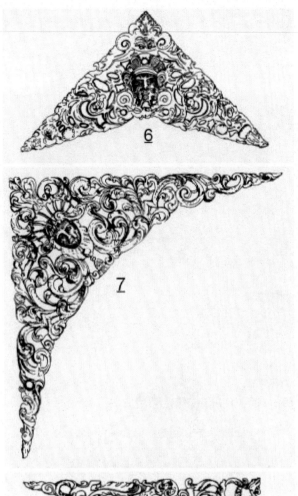

6. Used in London from 1700, and in the provinces

C 1725 to 1740

7. First appears in the provinces 1715,

very popular C1730 to 1740

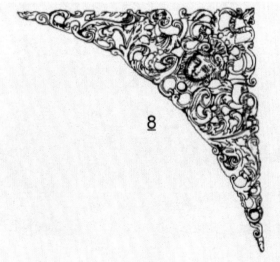

8. As above (7)

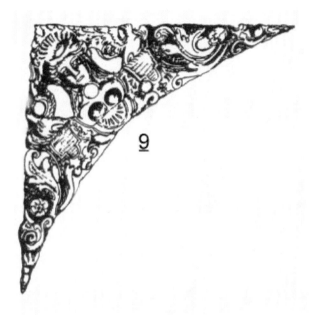

9. Very much used in the South and South Midlands on cottage clocks 1730 to 1750

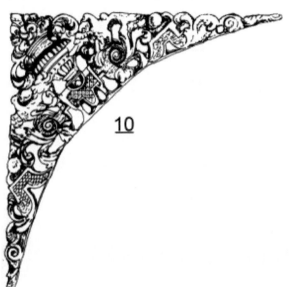

10. First known example 1709, very popular

1730 to 1765.

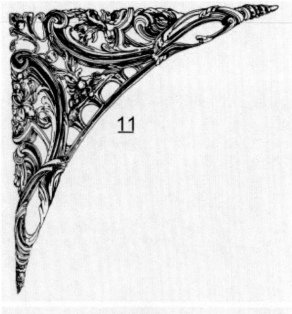

11. First example 1750, but much used 1765 to 1785

12. Provincial pattern, 1755 to 1780

13. As above (12)

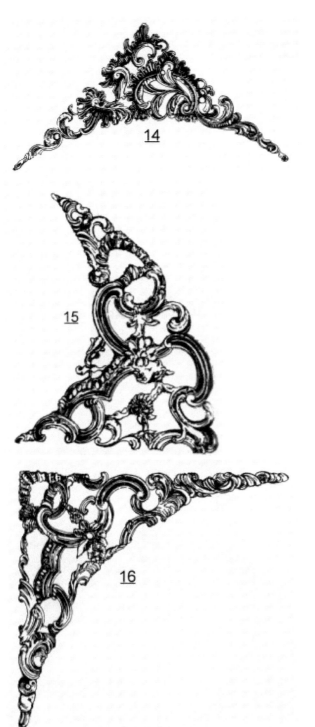

14. Rococo pattern, used 1760 to 1785

15. Arch dial spandrel, 1760 to 1785

16. Used together with (15) above 1760 to 1785

Painted Dial Clocks

Painted dial clocks are often called "white dial clocks" in Britain. Painted dial clocks appeared about 1765 to 1780, and after this the brass dial clock ceased to be made, again with just a few exceptions in rural areas, especially the far southern counties of England. The majority of English grandfather clocks were made in The Midlands and the North of England. The new painted dial was cheaper and easier to produce and easier to read by the poor light available at night, so the brass dial was dropped from production over a very brief period, for our purposes it is fair to say that no brass dial clock was made in the big clock making centers after 1780.

It may be worth a mention here that the clocks we are talking about were no different apart from the dial itself; everything else remained the same in both cases, only the dial changed.

Fortunately the painted dials then followed a certain progression as the fashions slowly changed over time, this means that we can usually date a clock to the nearest five to ten years. - - - And it also means we can see at a glance the important features without having to dismantle the clock.

White Dials

were first made in Birmingham, England in 1772. The first white dials from 1772 to 1800 were lovely, simply and sparingly decorated, and with much of the white background showing. Decoration consisted of spandrels painted on in gold paint in the four corners, (probably to resemble the cast brass spandrels fitted to brass dials.) Sometimes a swag of flowers or similar was painted on the dial face, but again very sparingly and restrained. The hands were made of steel, very fine, often blued or blacked and not exactly matching.

Another year indication of an early dial is the use of dots for the minutes with small Arabic numerals round the dial at 5, 10, 15 minutes etc. The hours are marked by Roman Numerals.

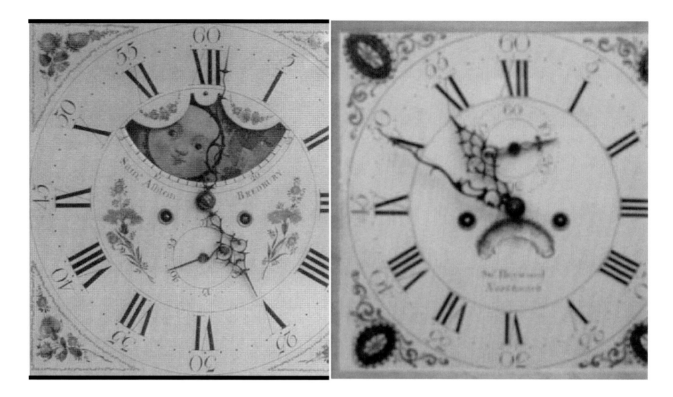

Two early painted dials, circa 1775 to 1780

From 1800 to around 1830, again the style of the dial changed slightly. The minutes were usually dots, and not the lines inside two narrow concentric circles that we are used to, but often the minute numbers changed to the quarters only, instead of every five minutes. The missing numbers were often replaced with little symbols, often looking like stars.

At this time it also became fashionable to use Arabic numerals for the hours instead of Roman numerals. The painted background decoration is starting to spread out too; arched dials have a scene painted in the arch, often with a spray of flowers on each side. The corner painting is spreading a little too, and the imitation spandrels are now often geometric designs, or a fan shape, or a floral design, which fills the corner.

Two middle period dials with Arabic hour numbers. Circa 1810 to 1820

Now we come to the later clocks, of around 1830 to 1880. In the North of England after 1830 grandfather clocks gradually got bigger and bigger, until by the end of the period some of them were huge - - - the dials were often fifteen inches wide and the clocks were eight feet tall, sometimes nine feet or more.

Given the larger area of dial to be decorated the dial painters went to town, the corner paintings became little masterpieces in their own right, and the decoration spread from the corner right up the side of the dial circle, to meet the next corner painting, and so on. Most of these clocks have an arched dial, and the artist painted in a large scene, often a biblical illustration, or a country scene, a nautical scene, a ruined abbey, or something ordered specially by the customer.

The hours have gone back to Roman numerals and stay that way; the hands are normally highly decorated brass and matching. These brass hands were used after 1830 for the rest of the period when grandfather clocks were made, in other words up to 1880, possibly in a few rare cases to 1890.

The minutes are shown by a minute band, two concentric circles close together, with lines inside to represent each minute instead of minute numbers. There are occasional exceptions of course, some makers seemed to have a favorite feature which they kept using long after everybody else had moved on - - - Date and seconds subsidiary dials are usual now, and the small ornate hands fitted to these are also brass and matching.

Two later dials, the painting filling the dial and arch. Circa 1840 to 1850

Another late dial, from the end of the Grandfather clock production days. Not much white left on here - - -

Center seconds hand and large date hand, rolling moon phases in the arch.

Very typical of the late dials, except for the center seconds and use of minute numbers. These may be used as seconds here.

Circa 1860 to 1870

To finish off, here is a quick guide to the various white dial features and their dates:

Some of these features can overlap, but looking at all of them gives a good guide to the approximate year.

(Of course, all dates are approximate, to the nearest ten years.)

Numbering

Dotted Minutes	1770 to 1800
Minutes numbered every five minutes	1770 to 1800
Minutes numbered every quarter-hour	1800 to 1820
No minute numbers	1820 to 1880
Roman hour numerals	1770 to 1800 then 1825 to 1880
Arabic hour numerals	1800 to 1825
Full minute band	1815 to 1880

Corner decoration

Flowers or fruit	1770 to 1800
Fans, shells or abstract	1790 to 1830
No painting - left blank	1780 to 1820
Gold imitation spandrels	1775 to 1785

Arch decoration

Name of maker	1770 to 1780
Flowers or birds	1770 to 1795
Small painting on white background	1795 to 1815
Full painted scene	1820 to 1880
Moon dial	1770 to 1830

Dial size

10" to 13"	1770 to 1810
13" to 15"	1810 to 1880
Square dial	1770 to 1825
Arch dial	1770 to 1880

Hands

Steel	1770 to 1815
Brass	1815 to 1880

FIRST AND LAST - - -

A very early unsigned 6.5" square dial, C1680   A very late 15" dial, C1880

.

SECTION TWO

The following is the repair procedure for grandfather clocks and many other clocks.

Leveling

Your clock will need to be level from front to back and side to side.

Place a small temporary shim or coin [about $1/8^{th}$ of an inch or less] under one side of the clock. If the tick-tock is worse, try the shim under the other side. Experiment with different thicknesses of shims until the tick and tock are even.

shim

Tilt her till she ticks with pride

Then adjust the crutch toward the high side

If it Still Stops

If the clock still stops when the tick and tock are even, there is one more basic task to try. Open the front and any rear door. Advance the minute hand to about five past the hour, pausing to allow any striking or chiming to complete, then remove both hands. Take off the pendulum and put it back on carefully. Remove the dial and try the clock again. One of these items may be binding. If it runs with these removed, put them back, one at a time until the problem returns, and you have likely

Correcting Beat

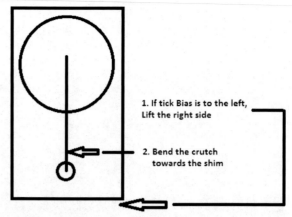

1. If tick Bias is to the left, Lift the right side

2. Bend the crutch towards the shim

found the problem. Study this area, track down the problem, correct and retest.

Lastly, test if it will run [faster] without the pendulum installed. The most frequent reason why a clock runs without a pendulum but not with the pendulum is that it is out of beat. It is much harder to move a heavier pendulum "uphill" than just the light fork only.

If still no luck, we will need to go to the next level. Most likely the clock will need oiling. The fact that the clock stopped is a good thing, it is trying to tell you something. If it continued to run with no oil, it would cause a lot of wear and damage the clock seriously. Consider the clock stopping as

"The oil light is on."

Oiling the Clock

We can try to oil the clock first of all without removing the movement from its case. You have a 50% chance this will correct the problem.

The most important thing to remember is to ensure that you only use clock oil. Using substitutes like WD40 can actually damage your movement.

Just like regular oil changes extend the life of your car's engine, regular clock oiling extends the life of your clock. Oiling your clock every five years will prevent expensive clock repairs and ensure that your clock will last for the generations to come. Imagine never changing your car's oil; it wouldn't take long for the engine to seize. Without regular oiling, your clock will end up requiring a major service, or possibly a new movement.

If your clock has a rear door, open the door to expose the rear of the clock. Remove the pendulum from its hook. **Never move a clock with its pendulum attached, or it will likely damage the movement.**

You will notice multiple oil sinks on the surface of the clock plate. Oil sinks are located where the ends of the steel arbor meet the brass clock plate. Please refer to the picture and diagram showing an oil sink.

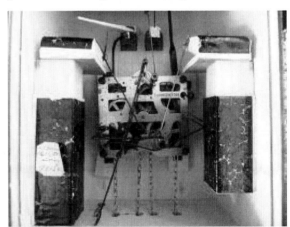

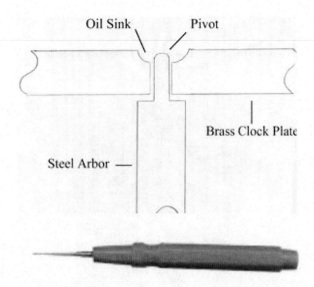

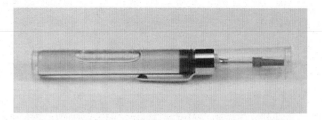

A better oiler is this Precision Dip Oiler

To oil a clock, apply ONE drop of oil to each oil sink. Use a magnifying glass to see better. Don't try and fill the oil sink, because the oil is held in place by capillary attraction and surface tension. If you apply too much oil, the surface tension will not hold, and the oil will run down the plate, leaving the bearing dry. Repeat the oiling process for all visible oil sinks. Oil the front of the clock with extreme care. Do not oil the wheel/pinion teeth during this process; they need to stay dry to maintain an efficient working condition.

If your clock has a front door, open it. You might need to remove the hands [see below] and the screws holding the clock dial on. When the clock movement is exposed, follow the instructions above.

below. It has a spade-like tip to hold a small amount of oil.

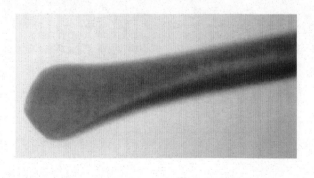

The eye of a very small sewing needle will usually carry the right amount of oil. Just wet the pivot.

It is best if you take the movement out of the
case altogether if you can. It is most likely
screwed to the case with four screws. With
the movement entirely out of the case, you
can blow out all the dust and debris with a can
of compressed air and then oil the movement
thoroughly, front and back plates, as stated
above.

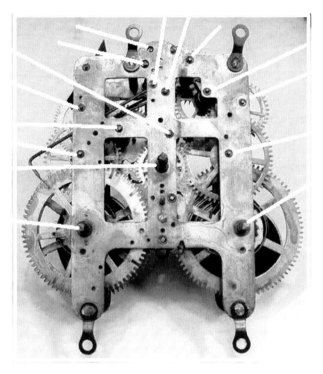

Do not be tempted to take the movement
apart at this point. Even if the spring does not
appear to be wound up, it is still likely under
some power. The spring can open violently,
causing damage to the movement and injury
to you. If you do want to take the movement
apart, please read this entire book first.

When it is all oiled up, put the movement
back in the case [not including the clock dial
and hands yet] and attach the pendulum. Test
the clock like before making sure it is in beat
with an even tick-tock. It should run now.
Let it run for a full day and then put the dial
back on and re-install the hands.

It is possible to clean the old oil and dirt off a movement without dismantling it. It is much preferred it be dismantled, but if you do not want to go to that level, obtain a water-based clock cleaning solution from

www.merritts.com, or

www.ronellclock.com or

www.timesavers.com

Place some clock cleaning solution on a soft cloth. Do not make the fabric too wet. The movement should not be flooded with a cleaning solution. You can make a clock cleaning solution by mixing eight parts ammonia to one part of commercial liquid cleanser, and one part oil soap. Use the soft cloth to rub off grease and grime that's stuck to easy-to-reach parts of the movement. Do not force the fabric into tight areas, as small pieces might break.

Dab some clock cleaning solution on a cotton swab or Q-tip. Insert into difficult-to-reach parts inside the clock movement. Rub gently to remove grease and grime.

Check the movement's wheels to see if they move freely, by gently manipulating the various parts with your fingers. Place a small amount of clock oil on a soft cloth. Clock oil is a unique product available from retailers. Do not use WD-40 as it may clog the movement. Lubricate only those parts that already have oil. Not all parts of the movement need to be lubricated, but those that do vary from movement to movement. Use the soft cloth to lubricate components that are easily reached. Put some clock oil on a cotton swab to lubricate smaller or hidden parts inside the movement.

Alternatively, soak the whole movement for about 20 minutes in the solution. After it has soaked, run lots of hot water over the movement to rinse off the cleaning solution and then dry the movement thoroughly using a hairdryer or in your kitchen oven. It is very important you get every drop of water dried off. Then proceed to oil the clock.

Pin & Collet

Look closely at the arbor of your clock on which the minute and hour hands are mounted. Use a magnifying glass to see if a metal pin is passing through the arbor, parallel to the clock dial. If you see one, your clock hands are held by a pin and collet.

Take a pair of needle-nose pliers and pull out the pin. The pin should be tapered, so pull from the fatter end.

Lift off the minute hand, then the collet. Next, lift off the hour hand. On some clocks, the hour hand will have a small clip or screw holding it in place, which you will need to simply remove.

Threaded Hand Nut

Look for a metal nut with a serrated edge screwed onto the minute hand. If you find one, your clock's hands are held with a threaded hand nut.

Undo the hand nut by holding the minute hand as close to the nut as possible to prevent it from accidentally bending.

Unscrew the hand nut with your free hand and lift off the minute hand, followed by the hour hand. Note that some clocks have a

slotted nut instead of a hand nut, which requires a special tool.

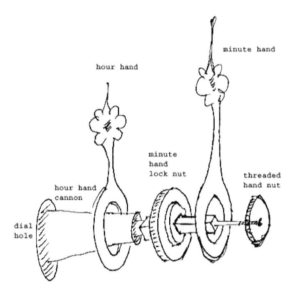

Friction Fit

Look at the arbor of the clock for a pin or hand nut. If neither are present, the clock hands are being held on by friction alone.

Grip the minute hand at the arbor and carefully pull it off.

Grip the hour hand and pull it off. Never try to pry friction fit clock hands off with a screwdriver as they may get damaged or the dial of the clock could get scratched.

Adjusting the Crutch

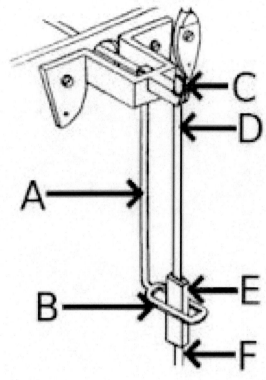

A: Crutch Arm
B: Crutch Fork
C: Top Suspension Block
D: Suspension Spring
E: Lower Suspension Block
F: Pendulum Rod

Once you have the clock running and the tick-tock even, you will want to adjust the crutch so that it will run correctly without the shims.

Identify the Crutch Arm on your clock using the diagram. Using a pair of needle-nose pliers, bend the wire a tiny amount in the direction you have the shims. Remove the shims and listen for an even tick–tock. Continue bending the crutch arm until the tick-tock is even without the shims.

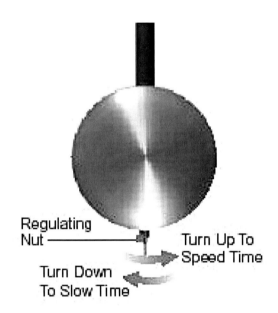

Regulating Nut ——— Turn Up To Speed Time

Turn Down To Slow Time

Regulation or the act of adjusting the rate or speed of a clock is a simple series of repeated steps until the desired effect is achieved. This is accomplished by governing the location of the center of gravity along the length of the pendulum.

While many factors may affect the timekeeping rate of your clock, none will make as much as changes in the ambient temperature of its environment. Any excessive friction from any source can have an adverse effect on the timekeeping ability of the movement. Every moving part must be in good condition and properly lubricated so the gear train can operate as freely as possible. Friction leads to wear, which is your clocks enemy number one.

Once you have observed a change in timekeeping over the course of several days, it is time to begin the regulation procedure. Keep a pad and pen handy for recording notes. Include the starting error, and all adjustments you make as this will significantly assist the process. Remember to use a rate of error that is consistent such as

minutes or seconds per 24 hours, and to use the same time source for making all of your comparisons.

Adjusting the pendulum shorter will cause your clock to run faster while lengthening it causes it to run slower or simply put "speedup, slowdown."

Look for the rating nut at the base of the pendulum, which is what raised or lowers the pendulum disk or bob. Remember that the pendulum disk may become wedged against the rod, especially in the case of a wooden stick, and some help may be needed. Turning the rating nut without affecting the disk has no bearing on timekeeping.

By turning the rating nut to the right, the disk will raise, which will make the clock faster while turning it left, will lower the disk, and make the clock slower. The rule of thumb is one turn of the regulating nut equals one minute per 24 hours, but your results may prove different, and that is what makes the note-keeping important to your success. By recording your actions, 3 or 4 daily sessions usually is all that is needed. You should not try or expect to correct the error in one session, but rather try to split the difference by half each session, slowly sneaking up on the error without overshooting or see-sawing back and forth.

It will not be possible to make the movement's timekeeping perfectly accurate.

If the above information does not get your
clock running, and you want to do some
actual maintenance to your clock, strip it
down for a full cleaning, repair wear, do not
despair, there is plenty more you can do. I
will walk you through it.

Above is a typical clock movement, and
below is the same movement dismantled.

I will use the following cottage clock, made
in about 1880, long before computers, before
the automobile was invented, in fact before
electricity.

Taper pin

To get to the clockworks "movement," open
the front door and remove the minute hand by

removing the taper pin, then gently pull off the minute and hour hand.

If the hands are not held in place by a taper pin or hand nut, they are just friction fit. They may well have been in place for decades and be hard to remove. If necessary, add a drop of liquid wrench and retry. If necessary, use a 'hand puller' or pry bars. Take two paint can openers used from opposite sides. You can grind slots in them, but often they work as they come from the hardware store. Place a slip of paper with a slot in it on the dial to protect the dial from damage from the prybars.

Next, remove the four screws that hold the face "dial" to the case. Be careful you do not damage the dial with the screwdriver.

By removing the three screws, you can remove the movement from the case.

Note, each clock is a little different, but this same process usually applies.

Carefully remove the dial and set aside in a safe place. You will now be able to see the movement.

Clock 'Fun'damentals

A crude clock needs three essential items.

1. Power – spring or weights.
2. Means of regulating the power to a calculated period – an escapement.
3. Means of viewing the results – clock dial and hands.

When you look at a clock movement, you will see a bunch of gears. We call them wheels in the clock world. What do they all do?

In a very simple clock, we have three wheels.

driven by the weights which supply the power to the intermediate wheel which runs the hour hand and drives the escape wheel. The escape wheel has a time regulator called an escapement and pendulum. A typical three-wheel train will run for about a day [actually 30 hours]. The large wheel of the great wheel [the leader] drives the [follower] small wheel [pinion] on the next wheel

[intermediate wheel] in the train and so on until you get to the escapement. We call the wheels T1, T2, and T3. [T stands for Time]

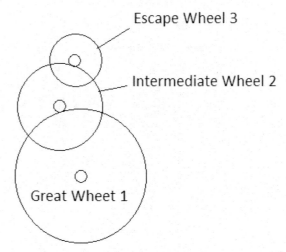

Three Wheel Train

Sidebar   A pinion can be cut from solid metal [cut pinion] or made up of steel rods [trundles or pins] in between brass ends caps or shrouds [lantern pinion].

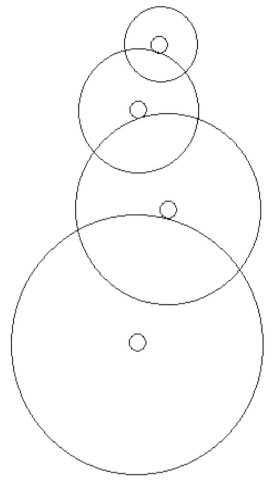

Four Wheel Train

If we add a fourth wheel it will typically run for a week because of the gearing. In this case, we have T1, T2, T3, and T4.

and if we add a fifth wheel, it will typically run for a month because of the gearing, in which case we have T1, T2, T3, T4, and T5.

This is assuming the clock is a 'time only' [no striking or chiming].

The rule for brass-steel combination is:
The component that will wear out is made of steel. In clocks, therefore, the wheel teeth are made of brass; the pinions are made of steel.

To add striking, we must add a second 'train' to drive that function.

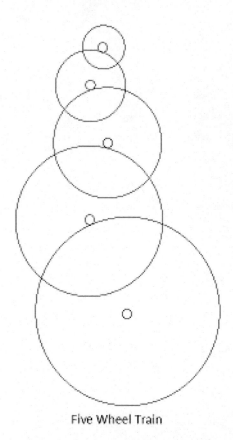

Five Wheel Train

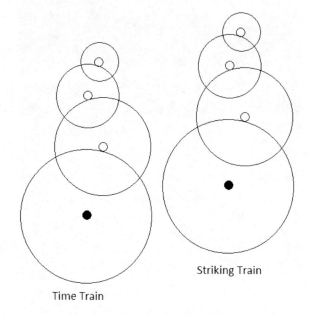

Time Train   Striking Train

This rule of 3 wheels, 4 wheels, and 5 wheels are only used as an example. There are many contradictions to this rule, depending on the teeth ratios.

Clock parts tend to alternate between brass and steel.
A steel pivot goes into a brass plate
A brass wheel teeth act on steel pinions
etc. etc
Why you might ask?

In mechanics, the use of brass-steel is called an ideal combination.
- Brass-steel requires no lubrication and is still wear-resistant.
- Brass steel knows no contact corrosion.

And if we add chiming also, we have a three-train movement that looks pretty complicated. But note, each train acts independently with only a lever that trips the next train.

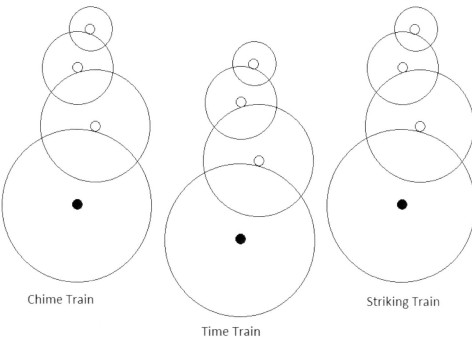

Chime Train

Time Train

Striking Train

Note the three winding holes on the clock below and how they match up with the arbors on the three great wheels in the above diagram.

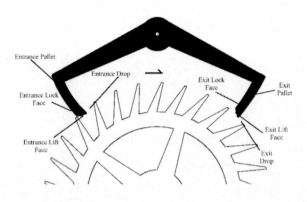

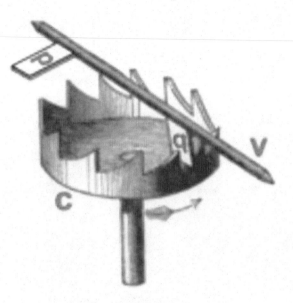

The job of the escapement is to regulate the time. Without it, the wheels would run wildly fast until the spring wound down or the weights hit the floor. The escapement will only allow the escape wheel to 'escape' one tooth at a time with each swing of the pendulum. The design of the pendulum determines how fast each tooth advances. Using calculations of the gearing, and the length of the pendulum, the clock is designed to it keep time as we know it.

Some people call the escapement a 'verge'. It should be noted that a verge is a very specific, old type of escapement that you are unlikely to come across. I suggest, to be most professional, you do not use the term verge unless the escapement truly is a verge.

Verge Escapement
C. Crown Wheel
V. Verge
p. and q. Pallets

The most common types of escapements you will encounter are:

Anchor Escapement

Invented around 1657, the anchor quickly superseded the older and inaccurate verge to become the standard escapement used in pendulum clocks through the 19th century. The anchor is responsible for the long narrow shape of most pendulum clocks, and the development of the longcase or tall case clock [grandfather clock].

The anchor consists of an escape wheel with pointed, backward slanted teeth, and an "anchor"-shaped piece pivoted above it, which rocks from side to side, linked to the pendulum. The anchor has slanted pallets on the arms which alternately catch on the teeth of the escape wheel, receiving impulses.

Recoil Escapement

Note the teeth are pointing in different directions.

The recoil escapement is less accurate than the deadbeat escapement but is easier to manufacture for less expensive clocks and the clock will continue to run longer when dirty, worn, out of beat, or with other poor escapement adjustments.

It can be made in either anchor or strip pallet.

Deadbeat Escapement

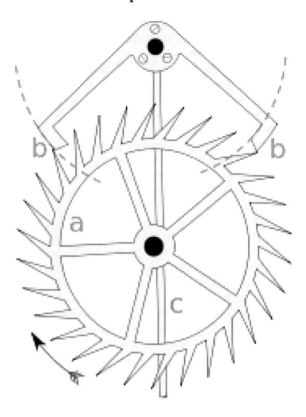

The Graham or deadbeat escapement was an improvement of the anchor. In the anchor escapement, the swing of the pendulum pushes the escape wheel backward during part of its cycle. This 'recoil' disturbs the motion of the pendulum, causing inaccuracy, and reverses the direction of the gear train, causing a backlash and introducing high loads into the system, leading to friction and wear. The main advantage of the deadbeat is that it eliminated recoil. The teeth point forward.

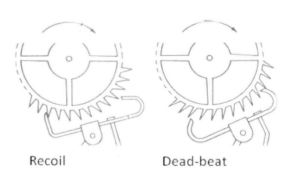

Recoil   Dead-beat

The **drop** on the entry and exit pallets must be equal.

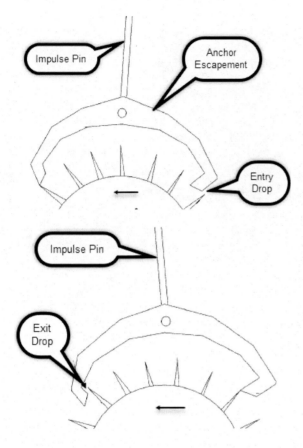

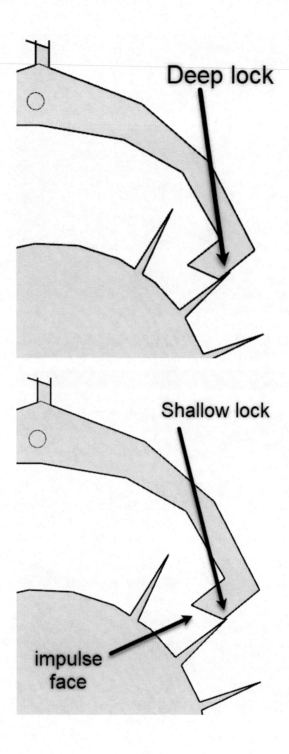

The **lock** on the entry and exit pallets must also be equal. If the tooth lands on the impulse face, more lock is needed.

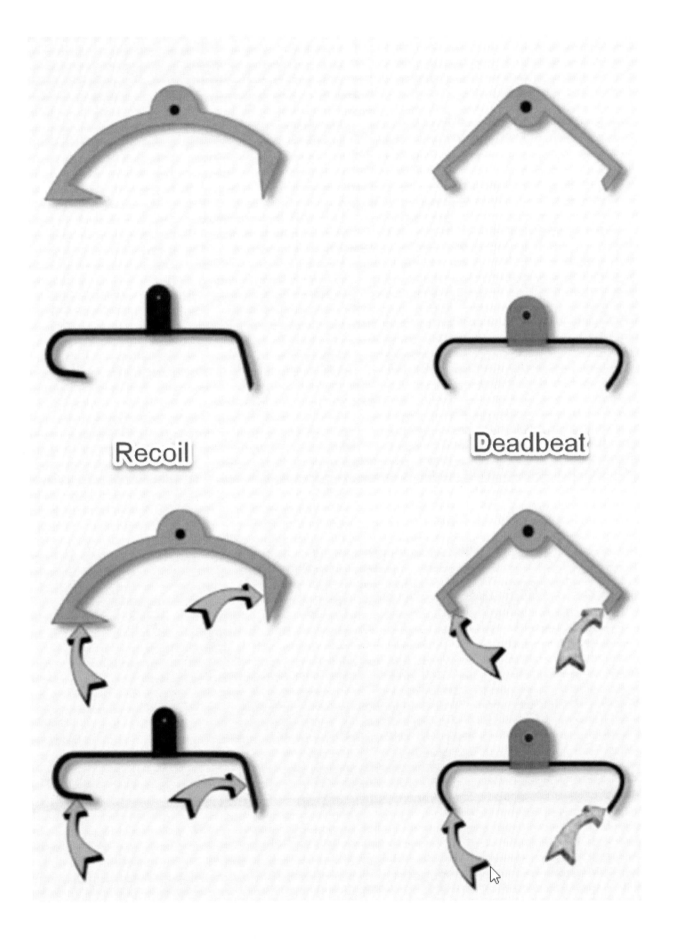

Recoil

Deadbeat

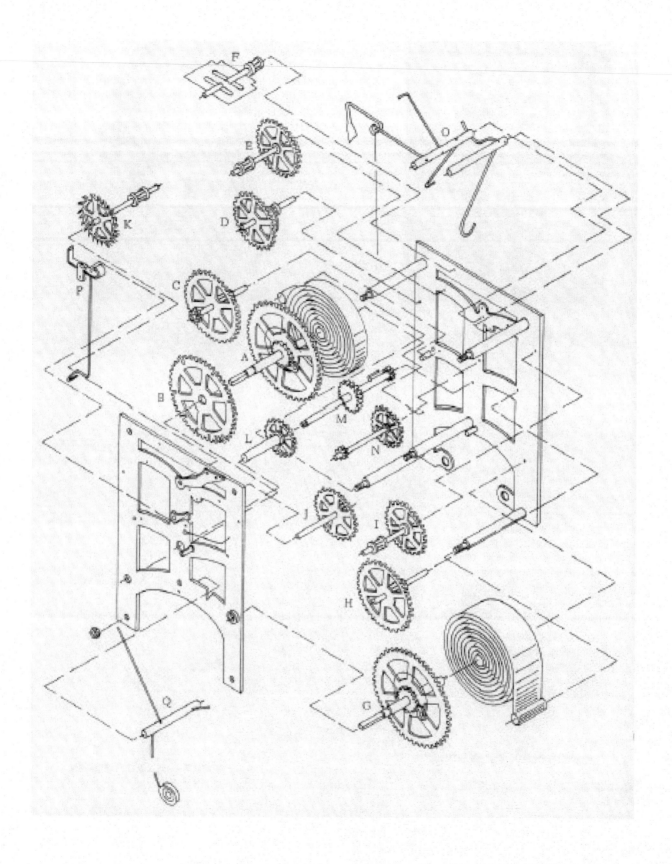

If your clock has stopped, you are sure it is fully wound up, and it is in-beat, there are two fundamental reasons it would stop.

1. Escapement Problem
2. Loss of Power

Escapement Problem

Look very closely at the escapement. If a pallet is 'hung up' on the tip of an escape wheel tooth, mark the tooth with a marking pen and restart the clock. If the same tooth is involved repeatedly, the likelihood is that this tooth is bent, or the tooth that has just left the opposite pallet is bent. To check and correct the fault, see the next section.

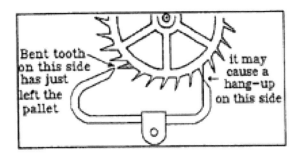

Loss of Power

If neither pallet is touching a tooth when you test its operation, that is, if the pallets are hanging freely between the escape wheel teeth, and if the pallets can be rocked without either one touching a tooth, and it is correctly adjusted as above, then the clock has stopped because there is little or no power transmitted to the escapement.

The Enemy

A clock is designed with approximately 10% additional power than is needed to run in perfect condition. This is to allow for a small amount of wear, and oils in less than perfect condition.

The enemy of a clock is friction. Clock oil gets 'gummy' or congealed because it tends to absorb the dust in the air. This gum will cause additional friction and stop the clock. The only way to remove the old gummy oil is to take the movement apart. I will explain this later.

Gummy Oil

A second problem is worse. The oil may have evaporated or run out, leaving the pivots to run dry, metal grinding on metal. The pivot connected to the wheel arbor is usually made of steel. The front and back movement plates that support the wheel/pivot are usually made of brass. You will note that brass is a softer metal than steel, so the movement plate tends to wear the most. This is by design, so the plates will wear and protect the pivot. The plates are easier to repair than replacing pivots.

This is an excellent example of why we dismantle a clock to service it. This damage was not visible without disassembly.

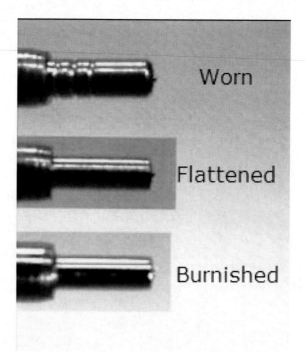

Worn

Flattened

Burnished

Properly fitting pivot

Badly worn hole in the plate

The pivot may also have some wear.

Imagine rubbing two pieces of sandpaper across each other. It will be hard due to the friction of the rough surfaces.

Now, imagine sliding two wet pieces of glass past each other. They will glide effortlessly. That is the effect we are looking for. See later for the procedure to create this.

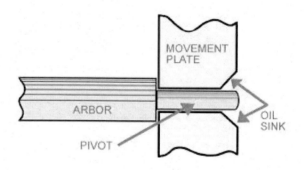

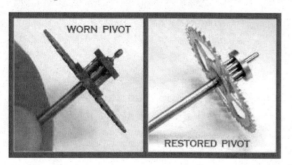

WORN PIVOT

RESTORED PIVOT

Escapement Pallet Wear

It is also essential to polish the impulse faces of the escapement. I have found, if you only do one thing to a clock, polishing the pallet faces will have the most improvement. Make sure you don't change any angles of the pallet faces.

The wear must be ground out and then polished. This is accomplished with a series of emery boards of different grits in a way that removes the least amount of metal and maintains the original angles. If too much metal is removed, or the angles are changed, the pallets must be reshaped or bent in order for them to be adjusted accurately once they are put back in the clock movement.

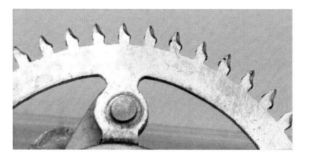

This wheel has serious wear to the teeth and will need to be sent out for a replacement wheel.

To track down problems, try a high-speed test by removing the escapement pallets and let the movement run fast. Watch very closely. It will often reveal bent or worn pivots, warped wheels or teeth meshing problems. Watch for it slowing down and speeding up.

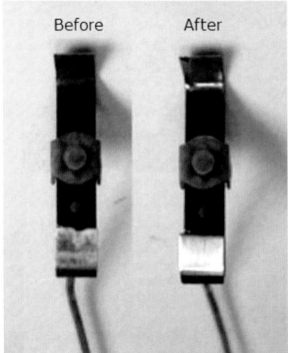

Before   After

Beginners Clock Repair Tool Kit for $85

[2018]

Getting started in clock repair can be intimidating, especially when you consider the tools that many clock repair people have.

I have created a list of tools that a beginner can get by with and do a lot of the work we do.

The fact is, 90% of what we do is performed with 10% of our tools. The basic idea is this list is well thought out, inexpensive and will get someone started without breaking the bank or putting you off getting started.

The First Set of tools most people will already have [or should have] around the house:

Needle nose pliers
Small square nose pliers with wire cutters
Screwdrivers slotted medium 1/4" tip
Screwdrivers slotted small 1/8" tip
Wet & dry sandpaper 500, 1000, 1500 & 2500 grit [available from auto parts store]
Cordless drill or Dremel [to act as a lathe]
Popsicle sticks or tongue depressors
Toothpicks
Tweezers fine and stout
Hammer small
Pocket knife
Empty containers and zip-lock bags for loose parts
Notebook and pencil
Small flashlight

Use a small fishing tackle box or shoebox to keep your clock tools together.

The Second Set will likely need to be purchased from a specialty house like:
Merrits www.merritts.com or
Timesavers www.timesavers.com.
Numbers are the Timesavers part number

Cleaning solution concentrate pint *17863*	$11
Clock oil *13839*	$ 2
3 Movement assembly posts *13408*	$15
Set of 2 mainspring clamps *20082*	$ 7
Letdown key set *15808*	$37
Mainspring Winder *13473*	$10
Loupe 2x, 5x *15870 & 18213*	$ 3
TOTAL	**$85**

The Third Set I call a "Bushing Kit" will be needed if you want to repair worn bushings.

Bushings 2 $4 each [Bergeon #7 & #9]	$ 9
Bush reamer [Bergeon #247]	$24
Handle for reamers	$13
Cutting Broach set .031" - .090"	$14
Smoothing Broaches .0314 & .0374	$ 6
TOTAL	**$66**

Note: I suggest Bergeon bushing. K&D are just as good, but they are not interchangeable so stick to one or the other.

Then we start getting into the more advanced and specialized tools, which can be purchased one at a time as needed.

Cleaning Solution

You can buy a readymade concentrate from the parts house [which is what I recommend] or you can make your own at home using the following recipe:

4 oz. oleic acid [Use Murphy's Oil Soap]

8 oz. Acetone

12 oz. 26% Ammonium Hydroxide

1 Gallon Water

Let soak for 5 minutes then scrub the parts with an old toothbrush.

Do not use laundry or dish detergent as a substitute for oleic acid. The detergent will pit, darken the brass in a variegated form, and will generally ruin the finish on brass clock parts.

Clock Oil

I recommend Mobil 1 – 5W-30 Its formula and viscosity are perfect for clocks.

Shhhh don't tell them, they will put the price up.

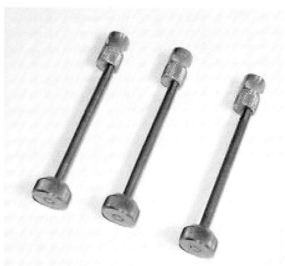

Movement Assembly Posts

You need these so that you can disassemble the movement. The movement should be disassembled horizontally. There are usually several items protruding from the plate, so it will not sit flat on the table. The posts raise the movement clear of the protruding items.

You can, of course, cut some holes in a small cardboard box and set the movement on that.

These are used to contain the mainspring while the movement is disassembled. Without restraining the spring, the spring tension could suddenly be released and cause injury to you or damage the clock when disassembling. 1-15/16" diameter is the most common size, or buy the set for a little more.

A fellow NAWCC member uses a toilet roll to support his movement – clock movement that is.

You can also use hose clamps instead.

Home Depot and other hardware stores sell Everbilt Rings:
1½" Nickel-Plated Ring [2-Pack] $1.55
2" Nickel-Plated Ring [2-Pack] $2.97
You will need to cut out ¼ of the ring.

Homemade Letdown Key

A satisfactory letdown key can be made from a 6" piece of wood closet pole [1 ¼" dowel] or even an old broom handle. Drill a hole in the end, then a slot to fit your clock key. The clock key will fit in this slot, and you can grip the pole to let down the spring.

stick with slit

winding key

I am not suggesting you never buy clock tools. The fact is many people enjoy buying old clock tools at marts and specialty tools from the supply houses as much as collecting the clocks they are used on. I own some tools I have never used, and some I don't even know what they do!

Check out my homemade lathe using a Dremel. I use it for quick pivot polishing, and it is very portable and does not take up much space. Note, I have added the three-jaw chuck to my setup.

Magnification

There are times when you need to see better than your normal vision, be it by the naked eye or with standard prescription glasses. If you use reading glasses, of course, you should use them for routine work. When you need extra help, we have several choices.

First, we need to define some terms.

Magnification – how many times bigger the object is seen.

Focal length – The distance from the lens to the object that is in focus. Typically, the stronger the magnification, the closer you need to be to your work. Some lenses have longer focal lengths than others, and the longer focal length can be easier to work with, especially for extended periods. There are times when looking at an object inside a movement, you will not be able to get close enough to get it in focus if you have a short focal length.

Magnifiation for typical Reading Glasses Diopters

Diopter	Magnification
1	1.25
1.5	1.375
2	1.5
2.5	1.625
3	1.75
4	2

Field of vision – How large an area is in focus at any given time.

Try stronger reading glasses. If you normally use say 1.5 diopter glasses, consider having some stronger bench glasses. Try the strongest you can find. Lope 2 ½ x, 5 x &/or Optivisor 2 ½ x with a focal length of eight 8 inches.

I keep a strong pair of dime-store reading glasses on my bench. I usually use 1.5 diopters, but for close up work, I find 4.0 or even 5.0 diopter work great and are easier to wear than a loupe.

Loupes have long been favored for detail clockwork. They usually don't specify the focal length when for sale. You will likely accumulate a variety that works for various types of work, and favor one that works best for you. Ideally, buy at a mart where you can try them out before buying. Loupes can be held in the eye, clipped to glasses or on a wire around the head.

A more recent choice is the Optivisor. They come in various magnifications and often have a longer focal length. They provide magnification to both eyes, and this also helps with judging distance, especially working with tools. They are comfortable to wear and can even include a light, but the light does make it heavier.

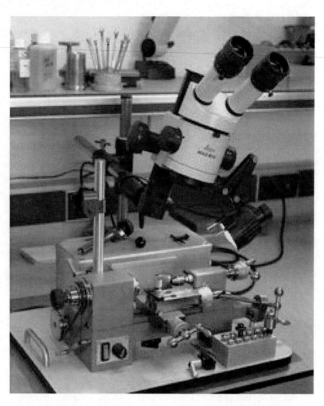

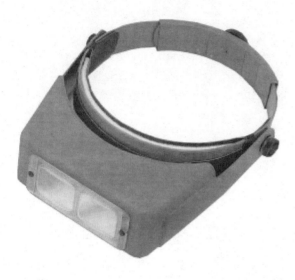

A less expensive microscope is the USB digital microscope. They are very inexpensive, under $40, and can magnify up to 1/600. You plug it into a laptop and view the image on your laptop screen.

This device will change your life and take your work to a whole new level.

More recently, the surgeon's loupe is becoming popular, but they can be costly. They usually have a longer focal length and a good field of vision.

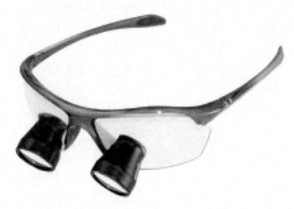

The ultimate in magnification is the microscope. This is most often used at a fixed workstation like over a lathe.

With the invention of the quartz movement, professional, full-time clock and watch repairers have almost become extinct, leaving a plethora of old and fascinating tools to harvest.

Tweezers

Tweezers come in all kinds of shapes and sizes. Long, medium, short, stout, weak, wide, fine tip, straight, dog-leg, cheap, steel, brass, and very expensive.

To start with, you can use household tweezers, but you will soon find they are not the best for our work.

For clockwork, consider Carbon Steel #3 *TimeSavers Item #: 33254*

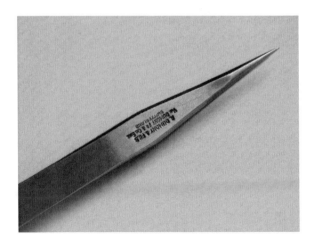

This is what I do to prepare my general-purpose tweezers. When worn, I will take 320 grit paper and with slight tension on the tweezers, pull the paper out towards the left,

then repeat pulling towards the right. Turn paper upside-down and repeat for the opposing tweezer tip. This is to give the tips "bite".

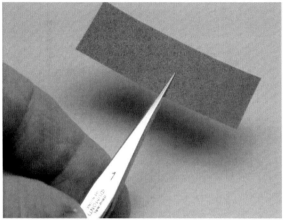

It takes a little practice to get hold of and keep hold of small parts even with good tweezers. You will often find that the part squirts out of the tweezers, across the room, never to be seen again. Consider adding a spot of Museum Wax. It will keep small items tamed.

Medical hemostats can be very handy also. They clamp onto the part. Great for inserting taper pins.

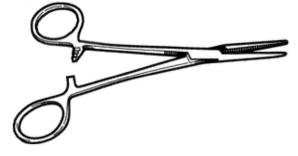

A More Comprehensive Tool Set

The following is a realistic goal to aim for

• An 8mm lathe, along with collets, a Jacobs chuck, and a 3-jaw chuck.
• A Dremel tool
• An Ollie Baker spring winder
• A bunch of mainspring clamps
• A couple of small bench vises
• A set of assembly clamps [assembly legs]
• A couple of small butane torches
• A soldering gun
• A 1" micrometer
• A dial caliper and a digital caliper
• Several homemade movement stands
• A beat amplifier
• The usual hand tools [pliers, screwdrivers, files, broaches, pin vises, saw, pivot locators, wire benders, letdown handle, drill bits, gravers, tweezers, anvil blocks, clamps, levels, and so on.]
• Various Dremel accessories.
• A small ultrasonic cleaner
• Adjustable swing-arm lights over the bench

Tools Conclusion

All I suggest is you get your feet wet first. I read a beginner book recently that contained 41 pages on tools. It is enough to put anybody off considering tinkering with clocks. I have amassed many tools over the years, some of which I have made myself and cherish them. My clock shop [more of a nook] is always a fun place to show off to visiting friends and guests who are fascinated.

the Clock of Life

The clock of life is wound but once and no man has the power to tell just when the hands will stop at late or early hour.

Now is the only time you own, live, love, toil with a will. Place no faith in tomorrow, the clock may then be still.

By joining a local clock club, you will develop friendships and contacts with experienced members that will likely work with you and allow you to use their specialized tools as needed.

Tempus Vitam Regit
Time Rules Life

Trademark of the NAWCC

The first thing we must do is inspect the movement for obvious defects. Use this checklist after you have removed the movement from the case and let down the mainspring.

- Look at the condition of the oil [gummy, dry, over oiling]
- Check the clickwork for wear
- Note any defects in the suspension spring
- Closely observe the action of the escapement with a loupe
- Make sure all the teeth of the escape wheel are correctly shaped
- Note any missing or damaged teeth
- Check for wear in the escapement pallets
- Make sure all wheels have drop [endshake]
- Check the pivot holes for wear
- Observe the mesh of all wheels to pinions
- Observe the condition of the mainspring [if visible]
- Create diagrams and photos of the movement

Dismantle the movement

- Inspect the pivots for wear

The following checklist will allow you to work efficiently without missing any steps. Perform the work n this order.

Repair Checklist

- ☐ Remove the movement from its case
- ☐ Make diagrams, notes and photos
- ☐ Contain the mainsprings with C clamps
- ☐ Dismantle the movement
- ☐ Remove the mainsprings from their arbors
- ☐ Clean all the parts in cleaning solution
- ☐ Polish ALL pivots
- ☐ Peg out ALL pivot holes
- ☐ Bush pivot holes as needed
- ☐ Test each wheel between the plates individually
- ☐ Final cleaning of the parts
- ☐ Put the movement back together
- ☐ Remove the spring C clamps
- ☐ Oil the movement
- ☐ Test the movement on the test stand
- ☐ Reinstall the movement in its case

To clean out the old gummy oil and to repair the worn pivot and pivot hole, we must take the movement apart. No whining, get it done. We need to perform our work using the surgeon's rule, "Do No Harm."

When taking off the pendulum, it is best to mark where it sits on the rating screw. Scribe a line across the top of the bob, on the pendulum rod. Assuming it was well regulated before you started work, this will save much time in adjusting the clock when you put it back together. Alternatively, place a piece of masking tape around the rating nut so it will not get changed.

If the clock has weights, remove the weights BEFORE you remove the pendulum.

Assuming the movement is already out of its case, we need to identify if the movement is powered by weights or by a spring. This is obvious if it is powered by weights, and they will long since have been removed and set aside. If it is powered by a spring, it is essential that the power be 'let down.' If the movement were to be opened-up while the spring is under tension, even just a small amount, the movement would explode, so to speak, as soon as the teeth start to disengage, letting the wheels run wild, which could cause injury to the repairer and cause severe damage to the movement. How we do this will depend on the type of movement.

If the spring is contained within a barrel [typically in European clocks], it can be let-down completely, and it is safe.

Spring within a barrel.

This wheel came from a clock that was opened up without letting down the mainspring fully. It has:

- Dislodged the wheel from its arbor
- Twisted the wheel
- Bent the wheel out of round
- Bent two teeth beyond straightening

If, however, the spring is not in a barrel, we must wind it up entirely and restrain it within a clamp.

To let down the power, you will need a letdown key. Select the fitting that is the same size as the winding square. You will hold the letdown key tightly with downward pressure and allow the key to slip through your hand under your control as you release the ratchet click. Make sure the clamp is in the middle of the spring.

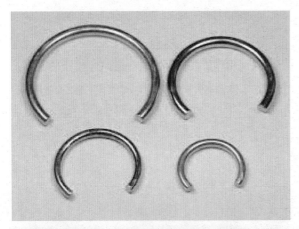

This can be a little tricky at first. It seems you need three hands. One to hold the movement still, a second to release the click and a third to hold the letdown key. Some options include:

- get a second person to hold the movement
- pop a couple of screws through the lugs into your bench or board
- hold the movement safely in a vice

screwdriver

Click

With the power let down or clamped, it is now safe to take the movement apart.

Dismantling the Movement

I strongly recommend you first take apart a junk clock that has little value and no sentimental attachment. The last thing you want to do is damage a family heirloom or an expensive Vienna Regulator. Ideally, start with a time-only movement, then move on to a typical American time and strike mantel clock.

Before you start to take anything apart, you must document the entire movement, step by step. Take good digital photos of the front, sides, and back of the movement [not the case]. Make sure the pictures are sharp, in-focus, and all parts can be seen. Also, make a diagram of the front, sides, and back.

Do not skip this step.

Take your time and make it as accurate as possible. Note each wheel and if the pinion is on top [above the wheel] as setting on the bench, or on the bottom [below the wheel] of the wheel PU or PD. Note the direction of the mainsprings.

This will not only help when putting the movement back together, but it will also help you understand the various parts of the movement. The springs and any barrels may look alike but do not get them mixed up. Keep the going and striking parts separate and marked.

If the movement has a striking train, making sure the strike is in the 'lock' position [just after completing striking] and note the position of all pins located on wheels or other places, and any cams, levers, and a rack or cam wheel. When you put it back together again, these all need to be in the same position. Note the name of each wheel [Great wheel, intermediate wheel, hour wheel, escape wheel, etc] and the wheel number – time side is T1, T2, T3 etc with the largest wheel being T1. On the striking side label them S1, S2 etc. [S is for Striking]

The Diagram

Many new students taking their first movement apart, are concerned they will not be able to put it back together. Others just jump right in without any study of the movement or documentation.

The best insurance you will successfully get a clock movement back together and run is to document the movement correctly. Slow and steady is faster. Having said that, I have seen some pretty sad diagrams that have insufficient information, and others that try to be a work of art, detailing all kinds of irrelevant details.

For this reason, I will give examples of good and detailed diagrams that do not need an artist's skill and has everything you need without any unnecessary clutter.

I will use the following two train movement with count wheel, as an example.

Sometimes the diagrams can start to get so busy it is hard to read. It is a good idea to create several diagrams, each with certain items you want to note.

Use a pencil with an eraser so you can make adjustments.

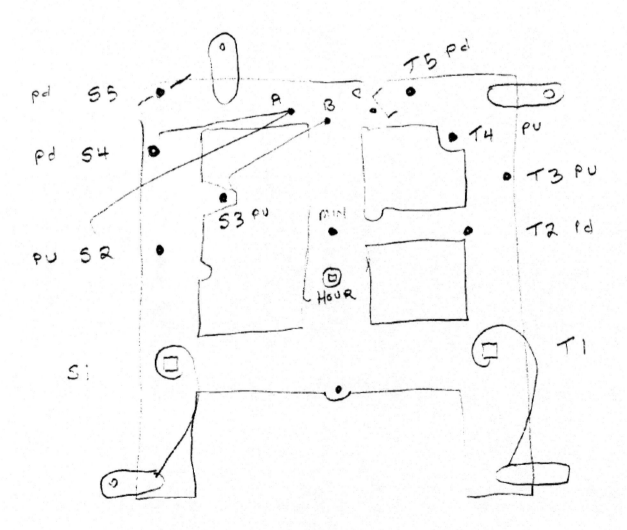

Next, make stick diagrams of each part. Orientate the parts in the position they belong. The vertical line is the arbor. The horizontal LINE is the wheel. The square is the pinion. Use whatever symbols you like as long as it makes sense to you.

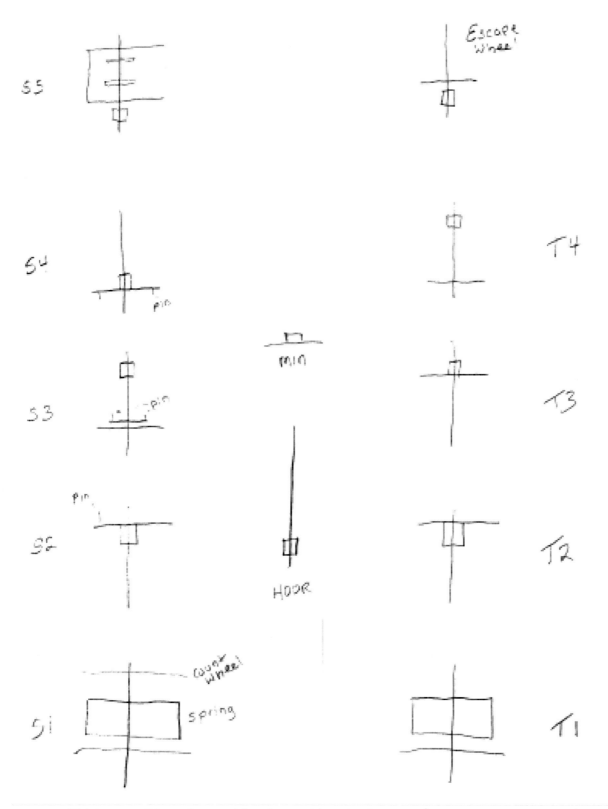

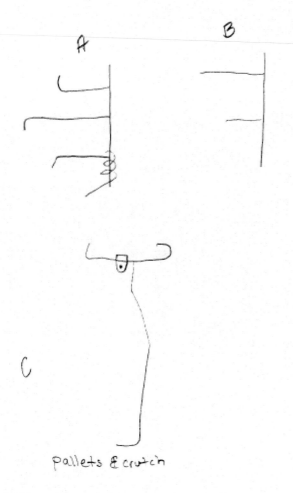

A   B

C

pallets & crutch

On your diagram, make notes of spring locations, pin location, and any damage you need to repair like:

- worn pivot hole needs bushing
- bent pivot
- worn pinion trundle, etc

As you get more experienced, the stick diagrams are not essential, but it is nice to always do it and keep them in a file in case you come across a similar movement later.

The stick diagrams are excellent for understanding all the parts.

Always keep records of your repairs i.e. where bushings are made, type of oil used, etc.

Descriptions

I will first describe the two trains so that you can identify each wheel.

Strike Train

I will start with the strike train because each wheel can be identified relatively easily [except the great wheel anyway].

S1 is the great wheel that contains the mainspring or the drum that houses the line or chain for the weight. It does not have a pinion but does have the winding click.

S2 [in this clock] has two pinions. One to drive S3 and one to drive the count wheel.

S3 has a cam attached to it.

S4 is the warn wheel, has the warn pin on it.

S5 is the fly that controls the speed of the strike train.

Time Train

After identifying the strike train, the remaining time train can most often be identified in size order. The largest being the great wheel, and the last wheel being the escape wheel with sharp teeth.

T1 First or Great wheel - is attached and ratcheted to the mainspring, or cable, barrel. The ratchet allows the mainspring or cable barrel to be wound without turning the wheel. The ratchet is called "the click". The first wheel turns the pinion of the Center wheel.

T2 Center or second wheel - which turns once per hour. Its pinion is powered by the teeth of the mainspring barrel in spring-driven clocks, and by the weight pulley in weight-driven clocks. Its arbor projects through a hole in the dial and drives, via a friction coupling, the cannon pinion, which carries the minute hand. It also drives the pinion of the third wheel.

T3 The third wheel - drives the pinion of the fourth wheel.

T4 Fourth wheel - This turns once per minute. The fourth wheel also turns the escape wheel pinion.

T5 Escape wheel - This wheel is released [escapes] one tooth at a time by the escapement, with each swing of the pendulum. The escape wheel keeps the pendulum swinging by giving it a small push each time it moves forward.

There are a couple more wheels for the motion works. The hour wheel has a very distinctive pipe that holds the hour hand. The hour pipe slides over the minute arbor. The minute arbor has a long arbor with a square end for the minute hand and the minute wheel, which is the only wheel with a cut pinion [not a lantern pinion].

The great wheels may well look identical, so it is best to scratch an *S* or a *T* on each wheel. On your diagram, make sure you indicate which direction the spring travels and where it attaches [usually to a post].

Levers

The most often place my students seem to neglect in the diagram and cause the most frustration on reassembly is the levers. Knowing how they fit between the wheels is invaluable. I suggest you spend more time on the levers in your diagram than anything else.

Wire Springs

There are likely several wire springs in your movement. These springs ensure the levers return to the ready position when not operating. Note the location, what it is tensioning, and how the spring is anchored to the frame.

Dismantling - Continued

Scrutinize the movement from the front and the back. Look at each pivot with a loupe or magnifying glass to see if there is any wear / elongated pivot holes. If wear is found, note them on your diagram, including the direction of the wear.

Sometimes you come across pivot holes with a double recess.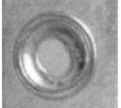

This is likely an effort by the original maker to work harden the pivot holes. This type rarely needs bushing.

Check 'endshake.' Endshake is a small amount of movement between the plates by each wheel. If a wheel were tight between the plates, it would add a lot of friction, so make sure the wheel will move up and down very slightly between the plates. Ideally, the endshake should be around 0.010inch. The fact is it can be more than this as long as the wheel does not fall out, the teeth all mesh correctly, and any striking pins still do their job.

Hold the movement horizontal, ie with the front plate up [with all the power from the mainspring clamped]. Keeping the movement horizontal, view each wheel to see if they have all dropped down onto the backplate. Then rotate the movement 180 degrees with the backplate up. Check if each wheel has dropped down to the front plate. Any that did not drop on their own have a problem. The great wheel needs very little endshake.

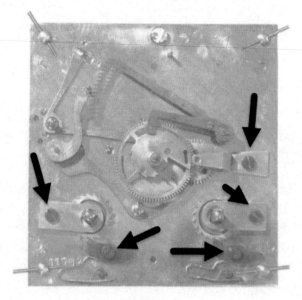

Take photos

If you photograph the movement from every angle, you will end up doing handstands and contortions trying to figure out where all those parts go when you get to the rebuilding stage. Photograph from the angle you will be rebuilding.

Clock movements are held together with either nuts or tapered pins, on the ends of the posts. Usually one in each corner. Remove the nuts or tapered pins and keep them safe.

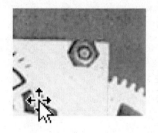 

Remove the top plate

With the movement horizontal, very slowly remove the upper plate in a way that all the internal wheels and components stay in position. Take another photo inside with the top plate removed, and make another detailed diagram. Make sure you include any levers in your diagram.

Items screwed to the front or backplates don't always need to be removed. Do not remove them at this time unless it is holding the front and back plates together.

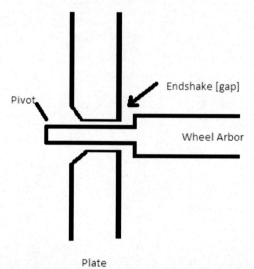

As you dismantle the parts, place them in a container, otherwise, "you may just lose track of time." String each train of wheels together in order on a wire. You can hang the wire over the edge of the cleaning container.

Sometimes you end up with a wheel that is press fit on the outside of the plate.

To remove them, reassemble the two plates so that the corresponding arbors aren't stressed sideways.

If you have a hand-puller, they will sometimes be helpful with removing it. If it is too close to the plate, you'll need something thin and strong to work under it. Ideally, you'll want to use two such tools or blades working 180 degrees apart from one another so that you don't bend or break the pivots. Small screwdrivers can work.

You might want to put a little masking tape on the plates, or slide a business card, etc. under the pallet wheel to prevent damage or marring of the brass plate. You may not have to twist the screwdriver [or whatever] at all. You may be able to just use it as a wedge to lift the part off of the pivot/arbor. Use

whatever pair of tools you have available which can fit under the part and wedge it up. Work slowly and carefully to lift the part straight up. Modified paint-can opening tools can come in handy in some cases, but if you come across a couple, save them. By grinding the tips, so they are thinner, two can be very useful in safely prying parts like this off their mounting.

If you don't need to remove the hour gear, you may wish to leave it in place. If you want to work on the pivots, and bushing pivot/hole, it will need to be safely removed. It may even come off easy.

Don't use a lot of force. Just enough to get things sliding and then ease up as the part comes loose.

The studs can usually be removed by unscrewing them, ideally with brass lined parallel jaw pliers.

Cleaning the Parts

The cleaning solution can be bought from specialty parts houses or made at home using the following recipe:

4 oz. oleic acid
8 oz. Acetone
12 oz. 26% Ammonium Hydroxide
1 Gallon Water

I have always been disappointed with the homemade solution and do not recommend it.

Let soak for 5 minutes then scrub the parts with an old toothbrush.

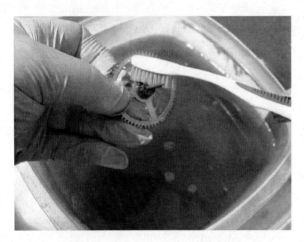

My experience is this formula does a poor job. The commercial clock cleaning solutions are designed specifically for cleaning brass, generally do not have strong ammonia smells, are safe and will not damage brass parts when used as directed.

After diluting the product as recommended, the cost isn't much different than the kitchen product alternatives. Some "dish soap" and other household cleaners [Simple Green and the like] may remove the oil and grease and dirt but can tarnish and turn brass dark on a long exposure. Ammonia and products containing the standard form of ammonia have a strong smell and have the potential to cause or worsen "stress crack corrosion."

Dawn dish detergent IS a good grease cutter but will not brighten brass. 'La's Totally Awesome Cleaner' is also a great grease cutter and very inexpensive. I tested it on brass for a pretty long exposure and found it less likely to tarnish the brass. Still, I recommend using one of the commercial products.

My personal preference is "Polychem Deox-007 Concentrate." It has no nasty ammonia odor, and one pint makes one gallon of cleaning solution, available from TimeSavers.

* A mildly alkaline blend for the efficient removal of oils, grease, tarnish, stains, corrosion, and oxidation from brass, bronze, copper, gold, and silver.
* It can be safely used in ultrasonics, agitated tanks, or manually.
* It provides long-term protection from tarnish, corrosion, and oxidation.
* Removes tarnishes and brightens metal parts.
* Use with water in a 7:1 water/concentrate ratio.
* No strong odor.
* Nonhazardous.

The gold standard for cleaning movements and parts is in an ultrasonic cleaner.

It's the same device that the health industry uses to sterilize surgical instruments. Ultrasonic cleaning is a process that uses ultrasound and an appropriate cleaning solvent. They can be spendy.

Ultrasonic cleaning uses cavitation bubbles induced by high-frequency pressure [sound] waves to agitate a liquid. The agitation produces high forces on contaminants adhering to substrates like metals, plastics, glass, rubber, and ceramics. This action also penetrates blind holes, cracks, and recesses.

You can use the same cleaning solution either in the ultrasonic cleaner or just by hand in a bowl.

You can buy a jewelry ultrasonic cleaner much cheaper, but make sure it is big enough to fit the movement plates and pillars and all the wheels.

I string the wheels together for each train on a thin wire and drape the end over the side of the tank. This saves having to fish the parts out when done. Use a teabag strainer for screws and small parts.

For extra dirty movements or parts, protect your cleaning solution by pre-cleaning. Carburetor or Brake cleaner, which is mostly acetone, works great, and the pressurized air spray helps blow away the residue. Best if you use the straw.

Some precautions should be taken during cleaning. Always wear safety glasses so fluids will not splash or flick into an eye from a brush. Wear gloves and old clothing.

Do not put two mainsprings, one on top of another while coiled in the same direction. Believe it or not, if they are coiled in the same direction, they tend to mate together and are very difficult to separate. Don't put a dial or self-adjusting anchor in the cleaning solution.

Mark all containers containing chemicals and keep the containers sealed unless currently in use.

Plan on letting the parts luxuriate in the cleaning solution as soon as you have taken the movement apart, so you can fully evaluate the parts for wear and defects.

Once the movement servicing has been completed and immediately before the final assembly, clean the parts again. Once clean, use gloves to handle the pieces, so the oils from your hands don't tarnish the bright parts.

It is a good idea to have two batches of cleaner going. Use the older cleaner to do the first wash. Use the freshest solution for the final wash. Eventually, this will become the first wash, and the new solution will become the final wash.

A word about lacquered front and backplates. The cleaning solution may harm the protective lacquered finish to some plates. I like to spray a small area of the inside of one plate with a carburetor cleaner. If the area turns white, it is best not to immerse the plates in the cleaning solution as it will likely remove the lacquer. In that case, just clean in warm soapy water.

Scratch Brush

If you have parts that are very dirty, in places that are hard to reach or have tarnish or minor rust, you can use a Scratch Brush. This is an inexpensive tool that contains a fiberglass cartridge that does an excellent job of cleaning the problematic areas.

Drying after Cleaning

After immersing your parts in the cleaning solution for 10-20 minutes and scrubbing with a toothbrush, the next step is to rinse all the solution off the pieces with clean, warm water, preferably distilled water. It will not leave mineral deposits like regular tap water. Follow with canned compressed air [or air compressor] to blow most of the water off.

Use a spray bottle and a bottle of rubbing alcohol [I use 91%] and soak the movement in denatured alcohol between the rinse and dry steps. Try not to asphyxiate yourself while doing this, for the alcohol vapor is somewhat poisonous. The alcohol will absorb any water left from the cleaning. Ideally, a final rinse in acetone gives good results.

When complete, ALL moisture must be removed from the parts, or they will start to rust. This is easier said than done. The most common method is to create a simple heat box. It could be a cardboard or a plastic container with a lid. Cut a hole in the top just large enough for a hairdryer nozzle to fit. Also, make some holes near the bottom for the cooler air to escape.

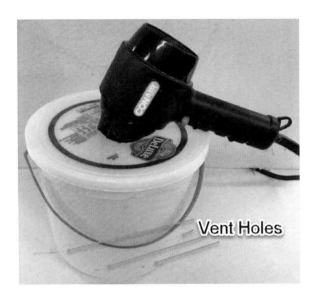

Vent Holes

With the parts inside the container, run the hairdryer on hot for about 10 or 15 minutes. When removing the parts, they will likely be quite hot, so let them cool before handling.

The parts can also be dried in a domestic kitchen oven at 180 degrees F for 30 minutes, but don't do this for any plastic gears or parts.

Pegging

Commercially available peg wood is either orangewood or dogwood, but good quality round toothpicks or skewers will work in a pinch. Pegwood is generally used to remove any residual chemicals or oils from inside the brass pivot holes, but can also be used as a burnisher to smoothen and harden the hole.

To use peg wood as a burnisher, hold it in a lathe, cordless drill or Dremel tool, and spin at high speed. When turned at high speed in a pivot hole, the peg wood will squeak as it burnishes the pivot hole and becomes burnished itself. Burnish from both sides of the plate, and replace or reshape the peg wood when discolored.

Using toothpicks as peg wood is faster, easier, and more cost-effective since there is no need to carve them to shape, and toothpicks are very inexpensive. When pegging, the toothpick will compress and even become dense enough to burnish the inside of the plate hole. And when the toothpick gets worn beyond use, throw it away and use another.

Use pegwood with a chisel-shaped end to clean the pinions.

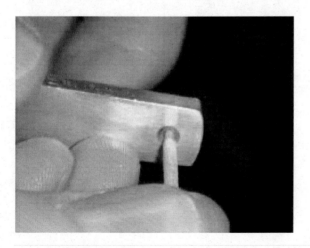

Making Repairs

The first job is to check the wheels one by one, especially noting any wear on the pivots.

The pivot should be perfectly cylindrical. After wiping and cleaning the pivot with pith wood, it should have a visibly smooth surface. Slide your fingernail over the pivot. It should slip along the surface, and there should be no grooves or roughness perceptible to the touch. Examine the pivot using a loupe [or strong magnifying glass] looking for defects. **It should have a mirror finish.** Place your fingernail up against the pivot, and you should see its reflection.

Note: the pivots must be corrected **before** pivot holes are corrected [bushed] because dressing a pivot will tend to reduce its diameter very slightly.

My homemade portable lathe consists of a cordless drill, clamped to my bench, and a second clamp to hold the trigger down while I use the drill. The keyless chuck is accurate enough for all but the most delicate clocks.

You can polish pivots without a lath at all, by holding the arbor in a pin vice and spinning it with your fingers, while polishing the pivot at the other end with a pivot file, resting on a block of wood with grooves in it.

I made my own Emery Buff sticks by gluing wet and dry sandpaper to tongue depressors in the grades of 600, 1,500 and 2,500. Lay out 4 or 5 tongue depressors side by side, spray with contact cement on the sticks and on a piece of wet and dry sandpaper and glue them together. Use a different grit on the other side. Cut apart when dry. Don't wrap the sandpaper around one stick, or you won't get the clean square corners that you need.

Only use the very course sticks [600] for badly worn pivots and quickly move up the finer grades, ending with the 2,500 grit for a very fine and smooth pivot. Finish with a semi-chrome polishing compound.

The drawback of this system is the abrasive sticks will tend to leave particles of abrasive embedded in the surface of a pivot that can damage the metals if allowed to remain.

Make sure you put the parts in the cleaning solution after polishing.

Burnishing

Burnishing is the polishing and work hardening of a metallic surface. This process will smooth and harden the surface, creating a finish that will last longer than one that hasn't been burnished.

Start by using a pivot file and a spot of lubricant. A pivot file is designed for the sole purpose of dressing hard tool steel pivots. The teeth are extremely fine cut, and the file is much thicker than any other of its size. The file will not bend when in use, and the edge is offset so you can get right to the root of the pivot.

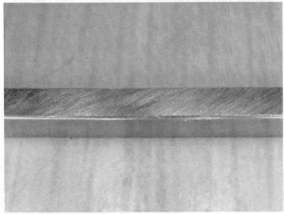

Once the pivot is flat and true, use a carbide burnisher to work harden the pivot.

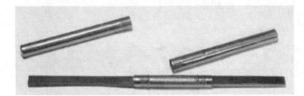

Lubricate it with the same oil that will be used in the clock to avoid embedded contamination, and with the lathe [or drill], turning very slowly, begin to rub the pivot with the burnisher from underneath so you can see what you are doing. Make sure you keep it flat on the pivot, so you don't change its shape. The accumulation of black particles forming on the surface of the burnisher will tell if you have applied the burnisher to the work flat against the length of the pivot. As with a file, run the burnisher over the pivot for the full length of the burnisher.

Apply as much pressure with the burnisher as you are comfortable. The pressure is good, but when a pivot is unsupported, it is possible to break a pivot using unreasonable force. A well-sharpened burnisher does two things. It cuts some metal away and is acting as a super-fine file. At the same time, it is compressing the surface of the metal to harden it.

As the pivot is being restored to shape using the coarse side of the burnisher, long, slow, deliberate strokes work best at between 500 and 750 rpm. Once the pivot looks acceptable, wipe the pivot and finish with the smooth side of the burnisher using more rapid, lighter-pressure strokes. Move the burnisher faster, but do not appreciably speed up the lathe. In other words, give the burnisher time to do its job.

An alternative is a 1/8" x 1/8" x 2-1/2" hard Arkansas stone with lubrication.

If a pivot is badly grooved, removing all the groves may remove too much material, weakening the pivot. In this case, I suggest you just soften up the groves, which will do little harm, reduce friction, and help hold the oil. However, you should focus your attention on the pivot hole to find the cause of the groves.

It is essential to polish the pivot shoulder also.

Pivot Polishing without a Lathe

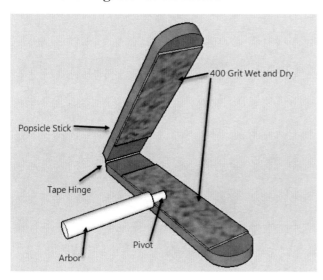

Glue 400 grit Wet and Dry abrasive paper to two popsicle sticks. Cut one end of each stick square. Create a hinge with tape so the tool stays parallel. Move the two faces of the tool together with slight pressure with your fingers over the pivot. Rotate the arbor back and forth with your other hand to smooth the pivot.

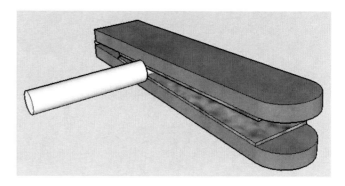

Make a second tool but use 1,500 grit. Use it, in the same way, to create a highly polished finish to the pivot.

I often get asked how to hold an arbor in a lathe when the wheel or pinion is so close to the pivot there is no way to chuck up on the arbor. First of all, never chuck up on the pivot [unless you are straightening the pivot – see below]. The simplest answer is to cut a thin strip of fine wet and dry sandpaper and run it around the pivot with your hands.

The correct answer is by using a Jacot Tool. Below are two homemade units. The wheel is fitted in a hole in the end of the Jacot Tool and the other end supported by a steady-rest. The wheel is propelled by the bent metal bar that drives the wheel arm.

My Jacot tool

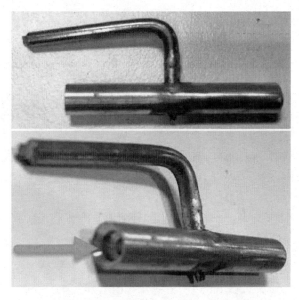

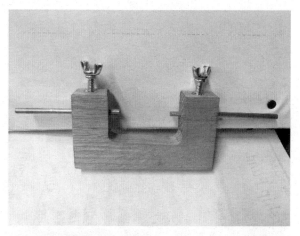

¼" brass rod that has a bent metal carrier [a nail] drilled and soldered into it, with a cone-shaped hole in the end to accept the pivot.

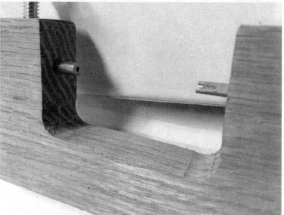

Homemade Polisher

I made this little polishing tool out of some scrap oak, about 4-1/2" by 2-1/2" by ¾".

The wheel sits between the centers. The left center has a hole in the end to accept one pivot. The right center has a hole in the end then filed ½ way down, so you can work on the pivot. The centers are made out of 1/8" brass rod, held in place by two thumbscrews, screwed into two threaded inserts.

With the tool held in a vice, the arbor can be rotated with the finger and use a pivot file on the exposed pivot.

Polishing and Burnishing Pivots and Pivot Holes

Burnishing is a combination of polishing and work-hardening of the surface of the metal. The smoother and harder the bearing surfaces, the less the friction and the longer they will function well.

Polishing

Polishing can be performed by any kind of cutting or abrasive device. Polishing powders, diamond compounds, stones, sandpaper and files are common.

A pivot file is most suitable for its ability to true up defects in the pivot such as barrel, bowed, tapered or cone shape as well as pits and grooves. The pivot file should be lubricated with the same or compatible oil as will be used to lubricate the completed movement to draw away shavings. Practice is needed to develop the correct speed and pressure to obtain the finest finish. Examine your work with high magnification. Use a back-lit micrometer to reveal defects in the shape.

With the wheel safely mounted in the lathe, bring the pivot file to the work carefully and purposefully from underneath so you can see the pivot at all times. Watch the pattern in the lubricant to determine where the file is contacting the pivot.

Burnishing continued

A steel burnisher when new needs to be dressed to make the surface flat and free of defects and the surface scored so it will perform its function. To score the flat surface, place fine [1,500] emery paper on a small sheet of thick glass and slide the steel across and back, creating a series of fine scratches, making it into a micro file. Make one side coarse and the other side fine. Burnish the pivot using light oil at high speed about 2,000 rpm to a black shine.

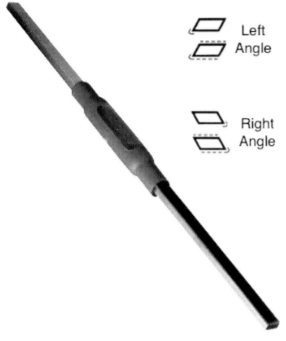

Left Angle

Right Angle

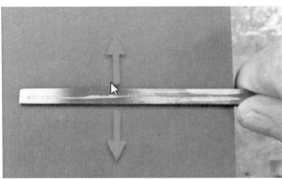

Use this lubricated burnisher the same way you polish as above, closely examining your work frequently and critically. Practice and practice. Not enough pressure will not harden the surface. Too much pressure will cause damage. Be sure to burnish the shoulder also as it will also contact the front or backplate. Be sure to remove the burnisher from the work, straight down to avoid damaging your work.

The finish you achieve will define you as a craftsman.

Burnishing the pivot hole

Burnishing the pivot hole is just as crucial as burnishing the pivot. Use a smoothing broach.

This is a tapered steel rod that needs the same prep as the flat burnisher. Fit the broach in the lathe, smooth it with 600 grit sandpaper followed by 0000 steel wool.

After pegging and installing any needed bushings, hand burnish the pivot holes with the prepped and lubricated smoothing broach from both sides of the plate using a light touch. When complete, remove any lubricant and carefully examine the back-lit pivot hole to be sure 100% of the bearing surface is shiny and bright.

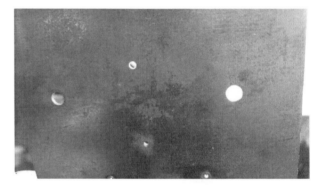

This is a good time to examine the pinions and clean them using pegwood to make them shine. If any rods need repair, see the later chapter.

SideBar

My son Jon age twelve, came home from Boy Scouts one day with a block of wood and some parts to create a race car for the upcoming Pinewood Derby. This was intended to be a father-son project. I was not familiar with this project but did a little research.

The next weekend we sat down to work out our strategy. I told my son the secret of making a winner was the shape of the car; streamline with 2/3rds of the weight at the back, making sure it had the maximum weight allowed. The plan was he would make the car shape in the wood, and I would help with the wheels.

An hour later, he came back with a design and explained how he arrived at it. He had taken to heart the 2/3rd rule and streamline, so we traced the shape onto the car, and I cut out the rough shape on the bandsaw. From there, he whittled away and sanded the final shape.

While he was busy doing that, I disappeared into my clock shop and polished up and burnished the axles that held the wheels. I also did my best to burnish the holes in the plastic wheels.

When the car shape was finished, I fitted the axles onto the car and mounted the wheels. My son painted the finished car, and we added some lead to bring the weight to the maximum limit.

On the day of the races, the car was inspected by the judge and approved for racing. I added a tiny amount of my best clock oil to each wheel. He won every heat and became the champion in the final.

My son was so proud of the shape he had created and 20 years later he still has that car proudly displayed.

I think he suspects that I had something to do with its success based on my clock talents.

The morel is of course - polishing and burnishing the axles and wheels made a big difference, and it will help your clockwork just the same.

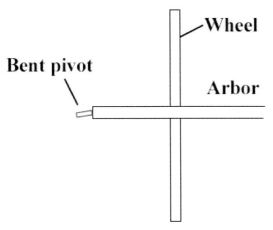

When you come across a bent pivot, you need to straighten it, hopefully without breaking it off.

First, you need to determine if the pivot has been hardened. Use a file to see if that arbor is hardened. Take a fine-toothed file and see if it will remove any metal from the arbor. If the arbor has been hardened, you'll find that the file just scoots over the arbor instead of digging in and cutting. If so, you can anneal it by heating it red-hot in a gas flame for a few seconds, and then let it cool down in the air. Retest with a file to confirm it is now workable.

Place the pivot in a collet in a lathe. Manually, [By Hand] turn head headstock. You will be able to observe the wobble. The high point and the low point.

With a peening end of a light hammer, gently tap the arbor to true it. Rotate it, so the high spot is on top and gently tap in a very gentle downstroke. This method will work with hard or soft pivots. This task can also be performed vertically on a drill press.

Be forewarned, it takes a learned touch and

very gentle taps. There is no need to reharden the part after the repair.

Another way, but this takes some skill, is to run the lathe at a very high speed and tap downward. You will be hitting the high spot. A series of gentle taps, and suddenly you will see the arbor/pivot running dead true.

For a bent arbor, again test for hardness. Place the arbor on a bench block or open vice and rotate it until the high spot is at the top and lightly tap it down with a punch until straight.

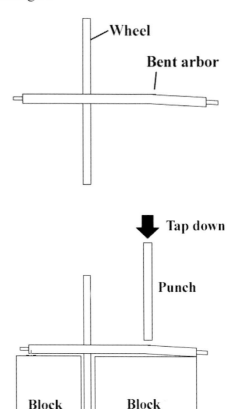

From time to time, you will come across a badly worn or broken pivot.

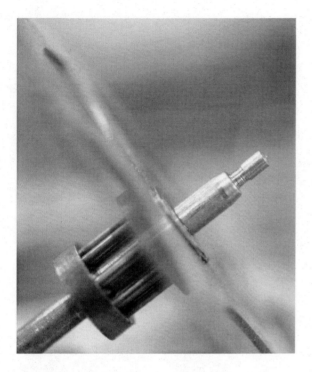

The only solution is to replace the pivot [or replace the whole arbor]. This is surprisingly a straightforward process, one that I enjoy, but it does require the use of a lathe [or a good drill/Dremel setup], a set of small drills, and an assortment of pivot wire. Most likely, the original pivot was formed by reducing the arbor diameter from a solid piece of material.

Use a file to see if that arbor is hardened. Take a fine-toothed file and see if it will remove any metal from the arbor. If the arbor has been hardened, you'll find that the file just scoots over the arbor instead of digging in and cutting. If so, you can anneal it by heating it red-hot, which shouldn't take more than a few seconds in a gas flame, and then let it cool down slowly.

Typically, the broken pivot leaves a bump that must be removed "dressed," so the end of the arbor is flat. Chuck a Dremel cutoff wheel in the lathe and hold the end of the arbor to the wheel until flat.

Chuck the wheel arbor in the lathe and chuck a drill bit in the tailstock. Use a drill one size smaller than the replacement pivot wire. Drill the end of the arbor to a depth of about three times the pivot diameter. Make sure it is drilled in the dead center of the arbor. I recommend using tungsten carbide bits. Frequently remove the drill to clear the swarf.

Insert the pivot wire with Loctite 638 retaining compound to hold it in place. Cut to length when set, dress up the end and polish the newly exposed pivot.

The new pivot should ideally be tapered a little to ensure a tight fit. Wait overnight before working on the new pivot.

Timesavers sells this Staff and Pivot Wire set for $7.50 and they work well for lantern pinions also.

Staff & Pivot Wire 37-Piece Assortment

37 piece assortment of 6" long hardened staff and pivot wire. Diameter ranges from .027" through .152". Made in India.

Base Pricing: $7.50

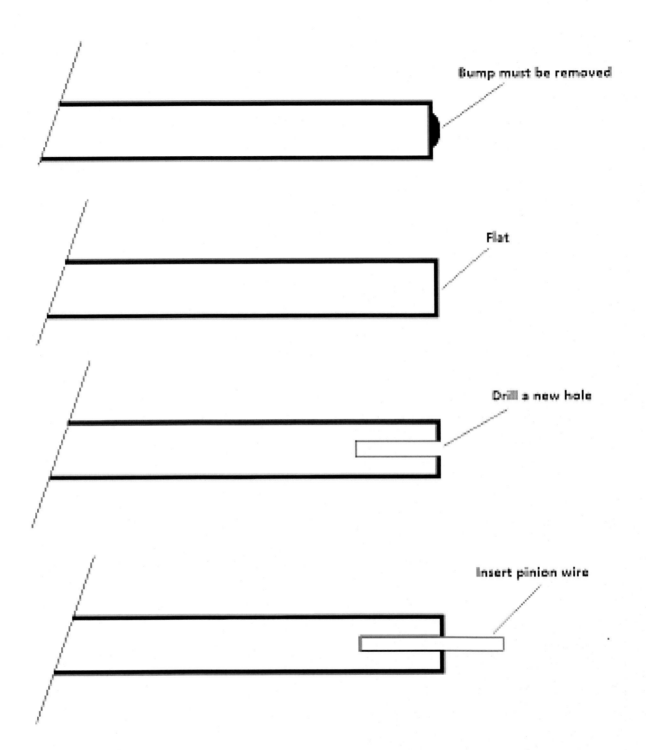

If pivot wire is not available, it is acceptable to use a portion of the back end of a drill bit, one size smaller.

With a Dremel cutoff wheel in the lathe chuck, take any remaining bump off the old pivot.

It is very important you drill the new pivot hole dead center of the arbor. You can use a centering bit [slocombe],

Or better still make your own centering tool.

Use a piece of ¼" brass stock. I prefer to use an octagon shape, but a round profile is just fine. Cut it about ¾" long. Drill a hole down the center using a 1/16" drill bit, then countersink one end. Now you can slide the countersunk end over the arbor. It will automatically find the center of the arbor. Use the same 1/16" drill bit to create a small divot in the end of the arbor, which will be dead center. Once you have a divot, you can use the correct size drill bit in a pin vice [or your lathe tail stock] to create the pivot hole.

Keep this drill bit with the tool. They are now one toolset. Only use this drill bit for making a center divot with the tool, nothing else.

Another method of re-pivoting a problem arbor is to install a replacement machined pivot end. The arbor will need to be shortened to allow for the new pivot.

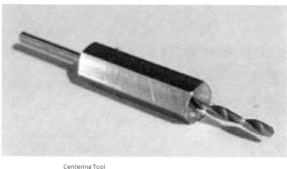

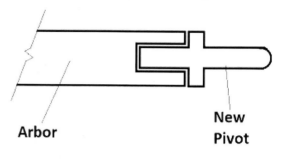

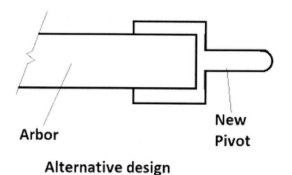

Alternative design

With the wheel in the headstock and a drill bit in the tailstock [or pin-vice], slowly bring the drill to the arbor and bore a new hole for the replacement pivot. Don't add any oil to the drill bit as it will interfere with the adhesive when we install the pivot wire.

You can use any of these Loctite products to hold the pivot. Clean the hole with alcohol before inserting the pivot.

Product Lists by Feature or Application	Top Products by Feature or Application
▸ Fast Cure	▸ LOCTITE® 638™ Retaining Compound
▸ High Temperature	▸ LOCTITE® 640™ Retaining Compound
▸ High Strength	▸ LOCTITE® 648™ Retaining Compound
▸ Close-Fitting Parts	▸ LOCTITE® 603™ Retaining Compound
▸ Loose-Fitting Parts	▸ LOCTITE® 680™ Retaining Compound
▸ Machinery Repair	▸ LOCTITE® 660™ Retaining Compound

Pivoting a Practice Nail

This is a 2 ½" finish nail. I used this because it is soft, cheap, easy to find and easy to work with.

A driil bit in a pin vice.

I chucked it up in a lathe [or you could use a dremel] and used my centering tool, just with hand pressure to find the dead center of the end of the nail head.

I put a drill bit in the tailstock, but it could be in a handheld pin vise.

After drilling the hole, I inserted a taper pin. I probably would not use a taper pin for a real repair, but it uses parts you will likely have to hand for practice.

When you need to bush a clock, it can be done either by hand or with a bushing machine. A bushing machine will cost about $900, and if you have access to one, feel free to use it, but I can bush a clock just as quickly and just as well by hand without the machine.

The following explains the procedure by hand.

What starts as a round hole becomes oval or pear-shaped. As a pinion drives the next wheel, it presses that wheel's pivot against the opposite side of its pivot hole. That's where the wear takes place.

You can see where the wear is, just by looking at the pivot hole. The rule is- *If it's round, run it, if oblong, bush it.* It's a good idea to use a marker to indicate where the wear points are before disassembling the movement. A good rule is if the pivot moves more than the thickness of the suspension spring, it needs repair.

When a gear train is turning in its normal direction, each of its pivots will be pressed against the wear point of its pivot hole.

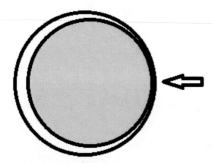

A well made pivot only makes a
small contact with its pivot hole

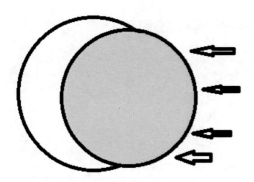

A worn piot hole makes much
more contact with its pivot

We call this oval wearing 'tunneling.'
If one pivot hole is worn, the other pivot will
be out of alignment and will bind on its pivot
hole.

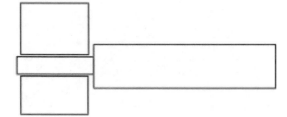

Well Fitting Pivot

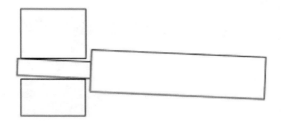

Worn pivot at the other plate causing binding

A worn pivot will also change the mesh
[depthing] of the wheel teeth to the pinion.

Correct mesh

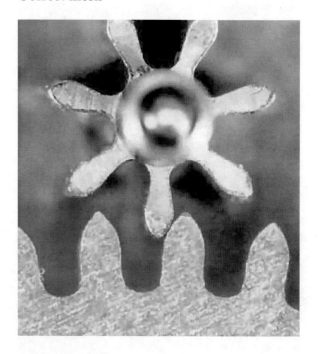

Mesh too shallow

Another way to check for bushing wear is to
let down the springs till they are almost all the
way down. Just a little power left. Then
watch each bushing on each side of the
movement as you rock the train back and
forth using the great wheel. If a pivot moves
back and forth very much [oblong hole] while
doing this, it needs a bushing. Mark the
direction of the wear.

The challenge is to install a new bushing with the same center as the **original hole**. The first step is to change the pear-shaped hole into a symmetrical oval.

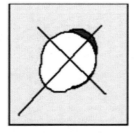

AMOUNT TO REMOVE WITH FILE

Determine [by eyeball] where the center of the original circle was.

To do this, let the mainsprings down into C clamps. Then wind the spring one half turn to give a little power to the trains. Now put reverse power on the second wheel back with your finger. The pivot will go back to the original side of the hole. By rocking that wheel with your finger, you can see the ware.

Mark the unworn side of the pivot hole with scribed lines and make notes of the ware.

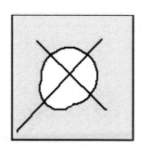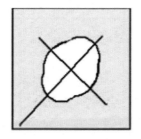

WORN PIVOT HOLE   **AFTER FILING**

With a small round needle file or Dremel, create an opposite oval identical to and exactly opposite the original oval, until you

have an oval hole centered on the original round hole.

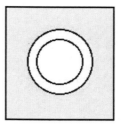

BROACH TO FIT PIVOT

With a cutting broach, enlarge the hole from the inside of the plate until it is round. A broach automatically centers itself in the middle of an oval. Since that is where the center of the original hole was, the broached hole is still centered on that point.

Continue broaching until the hole is not quite big enough to accept a bushing as a tight force fit. Make sure to keep the broach at a right angle to the plate in both dimensions, so the hole is straight through.

Select a new bushing that is the same thickness as the plate and has an internal hole just **smaller** than the pivot.

Use a reamer oiled with the same clock oil you will use when the clock is complete, that is made to fit that bushing, and cut the hole to final size.

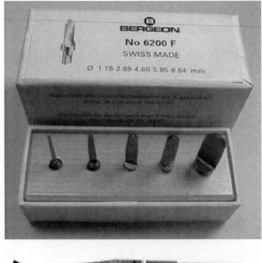

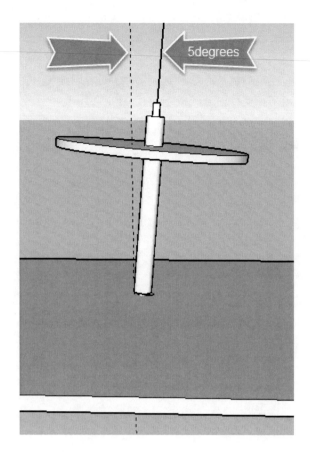

The reamer is a half-circle cutter, sharp on both edges. It gets gradually larger as you cut and press on the tool until you get to the parallel portion, which is the correct size for a friction fit for the corresponding bushing [3/1000th smaller than the pivot].

When you are just starting out, you can use cutting broaches instead of a reamer. Test the size often and stop when the bushing almost enters the hole for a tight press fit.

Lightly remove any burs with a countersink bit then install the bushing into the hole, from the inside of the plate with the oil sink on the outside, until it is flush with the inside of the plate. Use a small hammer and punch on an anvil block and tap it into place.

Use a 5-sided cutting broach to the inside hole of the bush, so the pivot perfectly fits the hole in the bushing. Then use a round smoothing broach to remove any roughness in the hole and work harden the inside surface. Allow five degrees of play. Slightly chamfer the inside edge of the new bushing.

Alternatively, if you just use a reamer instead of a file, make sure you ream out the hole centered on the original hole instead of the new oval. Insert the reamer with the round edge facing the side that is worn. Rotate the cutter ¼ turn left and back to the starting position, then ¼ turn right and back to the starting position. Repeat until the cut area is equal to the worn area, then continue cutting by making full rotations until you reach the parallel portion of the reamer. This is called nibbling.

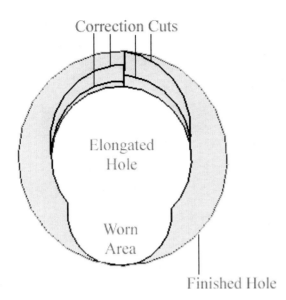

Correction Cuts

Elongated
Hole

Worn
Area

Finished Hole

Reaming out the hole will likely leave a burr on the plate. Remove this burr by gently rotating the chamfer tool, two rotations.

With the plate supported from the back, lay the new bushing on the hole from the inside of the plate and drive it into place using a punch or brass hammer. Smooth the bushing with emery paper, so it is flush with the plate.

Use a Dremel bit #100 in a pin vise to recess the oil sink correctly if needed.

When the bushing is complete, insert the wheel in between the plates by itself and test it spins freely and gradually slows to a stop. Then add the wheel either side to examine the mesh of the teeth to ensure the bushing is installed in the correct location.

One way that you can be sure of a good outcome for oval holes is to double drill the holes.

This is done by making a drilling guide out of an old hacksaw blade [or another appropriate steel strap] and clamp it to the plate in the correct, original position over the hole. Then

use a drill that just fits the hole in the strap to drill the initial hole and get it in the correct position.

Then, follow-up with the reamer you usually use for that bushing.

This is a good example of marking the pivot holes that need a bushing. The point of the masking tape indicates clearly the direction of wear.

Despite its name, the bushing machine is powered by a hand crank. Probably a better name for it would be a bushing jig.

Some say you must use a bushing machine to make sure the bushing is fitted perfectly vertical. I am not convinced of this. The final broaching is what must be perfectly vertical, and that is always done by hand.

The main advantage of the bushing machine is you can lock the plate to be precisely in line with the correct location of the pivot hole, not the worn location. Start by loosely fitting the plate in the clamps with the oil sink facing down and the inside of the plate facing up. Insert a centering point in the chuck, bring down the point and adjust the plate, so it lines up precisely with the original pivot hole with the centering point.

Now lock in the clamps.

If the pivot hole is worn oval, align the centering point with the center of the original pivot hole [not the oval], and lock everything down tight.

Next, insert the reamer in the chuck of the tool, add some oil to assist the cutting and rotating it slowly by hand. Bring it down to cut a hole for the new bushing.

Start with a small reamer and work up to the correct size.

Next, lightly use the chamfering cutter to take off any sharp edge. Place the correct bush in line with the hole, insert the pusher in the chuck, and tap the bushing into place with light taps of the clockmaker's hammer.

Finally, the hole in the new bushing must be hand opened using a 5-sided cutting broach to suit the polished pivot and burnished with a round oiled smoothing broach.

Finish up with pegwood to remove any dirt and debris.

Occasionally you will come across a movement with steel front and backplates. Steel plates are very hard on reamers. I suggest you predrill the holes just undersize and finish with the correct reamer. Use some cutting oil on the reamer, this saves wear on reamers. Use them only for the final 'few thou.' if at all.

Reamers can be redressed [sharpened] with a fine Arkansas stone. Put the flat of the reamer down on the stone and use a light machine oil on the stone. Hold the reamer down firmly and work it back and forth a few strokes. That way the cutting edge is honed without reducing the OD. This can be done many times without any degradation in performance.

Steel Plates

Benchtop Drill Press

An interesting alternative to a bushing machine is a small bench drill press and vice. You can do just about everything a bushing machine will do and a lot more with this setup for under $100. *Timesavers 10305* This one is only 12" tall with variable speed.

There is a Drill Press Bushing Tool Adapter available at Timesavers. A bit spendy.

Capture the clock plate with a 6-Inch Drill Press Vise, which can bolt to the base of the drill press or clamp it down to a piece of backing wood.

With the drill press method, I prefer to open up the pivot hole with a drill bit just smaller than the reamer, then finish up the hole with the reamer. This saves wear on the reamers.

This setup has many other uses, including pivot polishing. Lay it on its side, and you have a lathe.

Making your own bushings

It is quite easy to make bushings in the lathe from standard 1/8" brass rod, available from many good hardware stores.

Chuck up the rod in a collet with about ½" protruding. Face off the end, find the center of the end of the rod with your centering bit or homemade tool.

Drill the center hole just a little smaller than the finished pivot, about ¼" deep, with the drill bit held loosely in a pin vise. If the bit grabs, let the pin vise spin freely in your fingers until you can shut off the lathe. This technique will save many broken small drill bits.

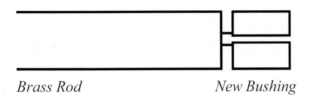

Brass Rod   *New Bushing*

Part [cut] the new bushing to length, just a fraction long. Do not part it all the way off just yet. Remove the rod and bushing from the collet and turn it around, so the newly formed bushing is held in the collet. Snap off the extra rod, face up the raw end, and chamfer the hole very slightly.

Slip a toothpick into the hole and release the bushing from the collet.

Drill a hole in the plate one drill size smaller than 1/8", dead center on the location of the original pivot center. Broach the hole until the new bushing just starts to enter the hole.

Slip the new bushing into the hole. Lay the plate, outside face up, on a heavy bench block, and using a round face punch, give it a sharp hammer stroke. This will lock the bushing to the plate and create an oil sink all in one process.

Merritt's also sells bushing wire. Long tubes in various diameters which can be more economical than buying individual bushings.

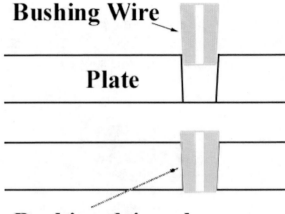

Bushing Wire / Plate

Bushing driven home

For the record, pre-made bushings are available in two grades, Bronze and Brass. Bronze bushings are more durable than brass, however, try to match the same material to the existing plates for fine clocks.

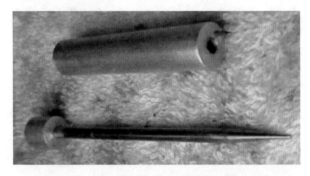

This little shop-made tool is excellent to permanently scribe a concentric circle around a worn hole. It also helps you make judgment on how good you are doing your bushing placement.

It is a brass pipe with a small hardened pin inserted in the end. The longer pin is inserted in the pipe to locate the tool at the location of the original pivot hole.

From time to time, you will come across [or create] a broken tooth.

To repair a broken tooth, use a sharp scribe to score a line from the center of the base of the old tooth on the radial line to the center of the wheel, no deeper than half the depth of the rim.

Use a jewelers saw with a very fine blade, set to cut on the pull stroke. Use only ¼ of the blade in your saw to give you better control.

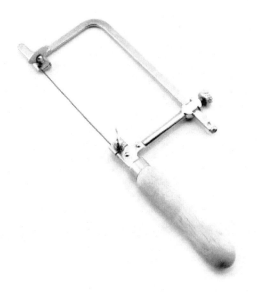

Cut into the wheel along the scribed radial line to the desired depth.

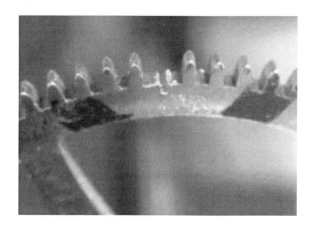

Cut out a dovetail shaped key halfway into the rim.

Using a very thin cut of 600 grit wet and dry cloth in a 'to and fro' motion with both hands will effectively smooth the base of the dovetail. Wet and dry paper will break doing this. The fiber backed type is ideal for this.

Finishing or widening the dovetail side is tricky in such a tiny space. My preference here is to use the cheap suspension springs with wet and dry paper glued to one side. This technique creates a tool that can work effectively in this small space and will not abrade other areas of the working space.

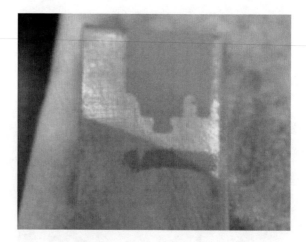

Once you're happy with your dovetail hole, cut a piece of donor brass, "clock making brass "C-353", place it under the dovetail hole, mask the wheel up with tape, holding the donor piece tight to the wheel with the tape. Other types of brass might work, but they will be harder to cut and fit to the exact shape. Spray the dovetail very lightly with aerosol paint and leave to dry.

Any paint on the wheel will dissolve in acetone. You will have the impression of the dovetail left on the donor brass, which will be a great help when sawing the new tooth. Leave plenty of brass at the large end of the donor piece for handling and holding in a vice.

The donor piece needs to be a tight fit. It is a good idea, with a very fine paintbrush, to apply a little solder flux in the joint before fitting. I use Tix flux [not anti-flux] and solder. This solder is very hard when set and will withstand the forces acting on the new tooth.

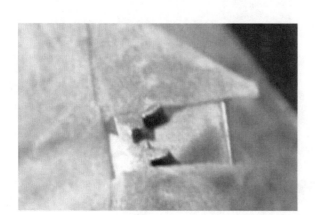

When you are happy that it will go in with a little gentle persuasion, a little tap with a brass ended flat punch will fit the piece squarely. Ensure there is excess donor brass either side of the wheel, and using a flat steel punch, 'peen' the donor brass to fit/fill the dovetail hole well. Do not hammer so much that the wheel is deformed, making it out of round. The flux has already been applied in the joint.

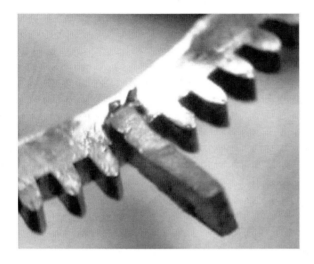

Place <u>small</u> chips of Tix solder on top of the joint. A mini butane soldering torch with a fine hot air nozzle from underneath does a great job. After it has cooled, clean off any flux thoroughly.

Cut the tooth to length

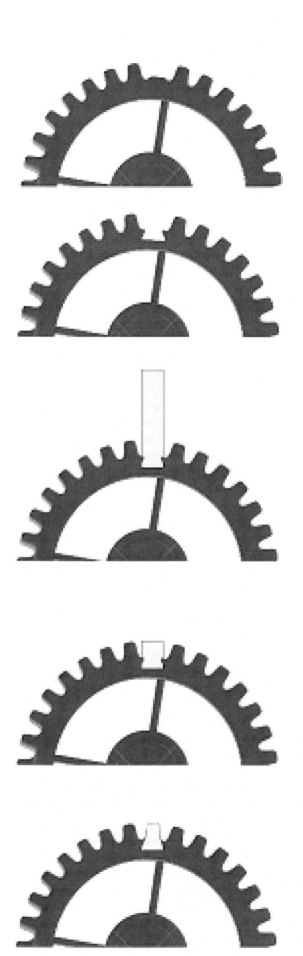

Slowly file the tooth to the correct profile, frequently testing its mesh with the matching pinion between the plates. Use a barrette file with a "safe edge" [an edge without a file profile] so you don't file unintended areas.

The dovetail can be carefully finished/polished with very fine wet and dry paper, to a point where it is virtually invisible to the naked eye.

When using files to shape the tooth, it is best to use as fine a file as you can, cut grade 4 and above. 'Escapement' files are smaller than other needle files. For shaping the top of the tooth, a Barette/safety escapement file is ideal. Good ones are not cheap and should be saved for delicate jobs.

An alternative approach is to find an old scrap wheel of similar diameter and tooth count. Cut out 3 or 5 teeth and its rim, and solder it to the side of the damaged wheel, matching the teeth even or slightly proud. File down the teeth as needed. This method can only be used if the mating pinion will allow the extra width.

For mainspring barrel teeth repair, you will need to cut out more material, as shown.

Rodico is available from TimeSavers for $5.00

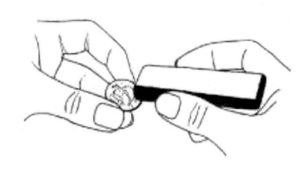

Rodico Cleaner

Description: Single 3" long piece of Rodico for cleaning precision parts, balance pivots, train wheel pivots, or for removing fingerprints and stains from plates, bridges, dials and hands. From Switzerland.

Item #: 14330

Rodico has many uses in clock repair, including picking up very small parts safely. In this case, I pressed some Rodico into the wheel that needs a tooth replaced, then used the imprint to make sure the repaired tooth is perfectly profiled.

This approach can also be used to solder a solid piece of brass alongside the missing tooth and hand filing it to the correct shape.

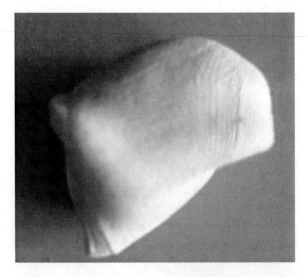

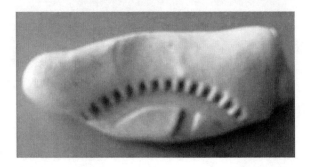

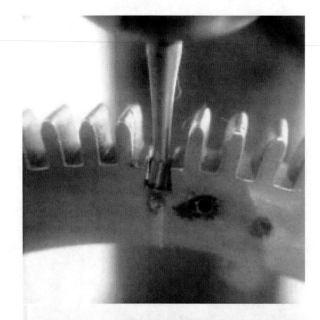

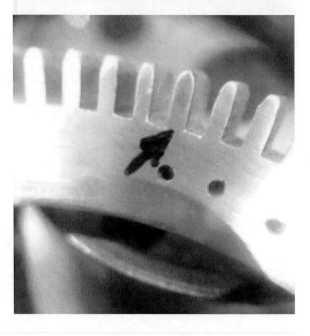

You can add a small amount to the end of a screwdriver to hold the screw while reaching inside the case to secure the movement.

I have not tried this myself, but dental 'burrs' have been used to create the dovetail shape for a replacement tooth. Search for "Dental Carbide Straight Handpiece Inverted Cone" Bur number 34 or 35.

Barrette files

Barrette files are machinist's files that are easily identified by the fact they are only cut on one face. There is a large, safe surface that is referred to as the 'back.' This means only one part of the file will cut a workpiece, leading to a high degree of security against mistakes.

Barrette files usually have trapezoid cross-sections, but sometimes they may be triangular, and taper in both width and thickness, which allows them to access small spaces.

They are double-cut, but only on the flat face. The uncut face is referred to as the 'back.' This means that they can be used for filing keyways, internal angles in slots and for general finishing and deburring, without fear of accidental wear to another surface during the filing process.

When combined with their taper, the fact that only one of their faces is cut makes them perfect for precision filing.

The Coarseness Rating ranges from #00 the coarsest, to #6 the finest.

To clean any file, rub a piece of copper over it. An offcut of copper pipe is just fine. Copper is soft enough to form grooves in it the shape of the file grooves, which then clean out the file grooves.

A lantern pinion consists of two end caps called shrouds, with hard metal rods or pins called trundles fitted around in a circle creating a very efficient and cost-effective pinion.

It can often be found that these rods are worn, bent, broken, or missing.

To replace one trundle, take a small drill bit, about #55 [0.052"] fitted in a pin vice and turn it by hand in the end hole to release the brass that is riveting it in place. It only takes a few turns to remove the soft brass.

The rods should be loosely fitted, so the first step is to rotate the rod to a new position.

It is not hard to replace the rods, but I recommend you do not take the whole thing apart at one time. They can be challenging to get back together again. Instead, replace each trundle one at a time as needed, and the job is quite easy.

Once it is released, you can slide the trundle out using needle-nose pliers.

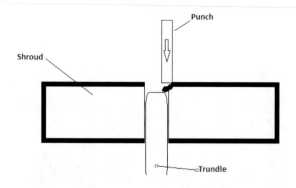

Find a pivot wire that is the correct size, cut it to length using a Dremel cutoff wheel, leaving room to rivet [swage] it back in and close the hole a little with a small punch.

It is important to support the upper shroud, or it might slide down when riveting.

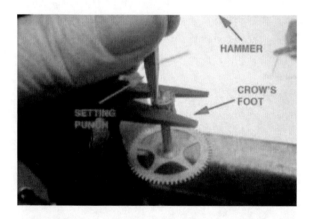

This pair of needle nose pliers have been modified. The bottom jaw a was slotted with a Dremel tool and cutoff blade. The top was heated, bent and ground to shape as shown. It will support the shroud and close the hole in one motion.

An alternative is to hold it in place using Loctite. The disadvantage of this method is it does not allow the trundle to roll when in operation.

Timesavers sells this drill bit set for $6.50, and they work well for many repair projects, including re-pivoting. *#17531*

second piece of pegwood with a slot in it to polish the tops of the leaves. If rusted, use a scratch brush or soft wire wheel in a Dremel tool.

Another option is to secure a washer to the top of the shroud, to hold all the trundles in place.

You might come across a clock with 'rolling pinions.' In this case, the trundles have a pivot formed on the ends, and they rotate between the shrouds as the clock wheel teeth pass by, allowing less friction and wear.

If you have solid leaf pinions that are badly worn, it is best to move the wheel down the arbor a little way, so the wheel falls on a sound part of the pinion. There is usually plenty of room to do this. If this is not possible, a new pinion will need to be made by a specialist company.

Very dirty or rusted pinions can be cleaned using pegwood with a chisel end formed with a knife to clean the bottom of the leaves. If needed, use a polishing compound. Cut a

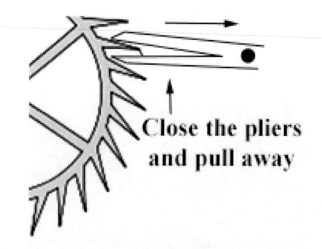

Close the pliers and pull away

Using a good pair of pliers with smooth jaws [no serrations on the inside face], carefully grasp each tooth at its root and gently squeezing, 'draw' the pliers out at the correct angle to straighten and stretch the tooth. This needs to be done with great care while the wheel is out of the movement. It will correct any bends and smooth out any imperfections. Every tooth on the escape wheel must be in 'perfect' condition.

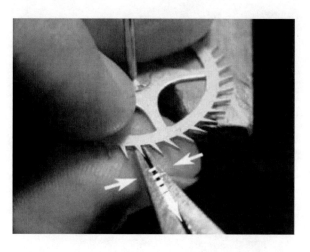

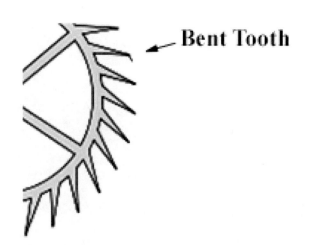

← **Bent Tooth**

After straightening teeth, the wheel will likely need topping to make sure all teeth are the same length and perfectly round. Use a lathe [or drill] and very light strokes of a fine buffing stick.

After topping, the backs of the fat teeth will need filing down to between 0.1mm and 0.2mm and make all the spaces between the teeth equal. Create a simple gauge to test the gaps. Press several known good teeth into Rodico to make an impression, then compare this impression to suspect teeth.

Make sure the escapement is properly adjusted. Each tooth should only just clear the pallet. The drop should not exceed $1/6^{th}$ of the distance between teeth. Check with a feeler gauge. A loud tick or a large drop indicates it is adjusted too far away. Adjust it closer until it catches the tooth, then back it off a fraction until it just clears.

Look closely at the escapement pivots. They should not move from side to side when operating. If it does, the offending pivot hole needs repair.

For the escapement to work correctly, everything about it must be in good working order. If there is any play in the saddle pivot, it will give inconsistent and thus poor performance. For this reason, we should pay close attention to the condition of the saddle pivot and its pivot hole.

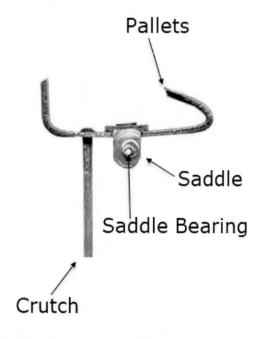

The saddle is not suited to bushing. If there is excessive wear, the saddle pin must be replaced.

To begin, the saddle pivot is removed from the saddle cock.

This can be done by securely grasping the pivot with pliers and pulling out while rotating it alternately clockwise and counterclockwise.

Another method is to use a pair of diagonal cutters [wire cutters]. Grip the pivot with the cutter close to the saddle cock and push downward on the handle. This will cause the pivot to move up and out of the cock.

If more leverage is needed, place the blade of a small screwdriver under the pivot point of the pliers, between the cutter blade and the cock. This will effectively provide a greater lever arm.

Next, measure the diameter of the pivot. For discussion, let's say it measures 0.042" diameter. Choose a piece of pinion wire several thousandths larger – about 0.045" diameter.

Test fit this larger wire in the saddle bearing. This wire should not be able to fit into the saddle bearing. Cut the selected wire to the same length as the original pivot. Now insert this new pivot into the hole in the saddle cock. It may be necessary to broach out the hole in the saddle cock to drive the new pivot tight into the hole. Be careful so as not to end up with too large of a hole in the saddle cock. It needs to be friction tight.

It may be necessary to swivel the saddle cock about its rivet to achieve working clearance to drive in the new pivot. If this is needed, make a small scribe on the plate to mark its position before swiveling.

After installing the new saddle pivot, the saddle bearing needs to be realigned back to its correct position on the scribe. Do this carefully. Check to ensure there is no burr on the end of the new pivot. If there is, file it smooth.

Broach the outboard saddle bearing first to achieve a good pivot-fit. Then flip the saddle unit over and broach the inboard bearing. DO NOT attempt broaching through the outboard bearing to broach the inboard bearing, the taper of the broach will cause the outboard bearing to be too large, when a good fit is achieved for the inboard bearing.

Once a good fit is achieved, place the saddle on the saddle pivot and secure with the retainer. Lubricate both the inboard and outboard saddle bearing. Hold the clock plate in a plum position and give the crutch a swing to test for a good fit. Ensure there is no binding in the escapement swing. If necessary, re-broach the appropriate bearing.

This completes the worn saddle pivot repair.

As you dismantle a movement, you might find a broken or even missing spring that keeps a striking wire in its correct location. It is easy to make a new spring. Purchase Wire-Brass Spring #28 [*timesavers #23908*].

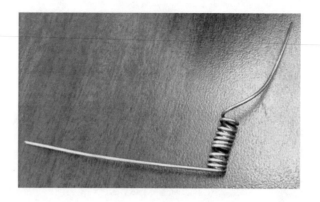

Cut off about 8". Starting 1" from the end, coil the wire carefully around a screwdriver acting as a mandrel, making sure not to overlap the coils. Stop one inch from the other end, then shape a hook at each end around the tip of needle-nose pliers, and there you have a custom-made spring.

If you want to get fancier, this is a homemade spring making machine.

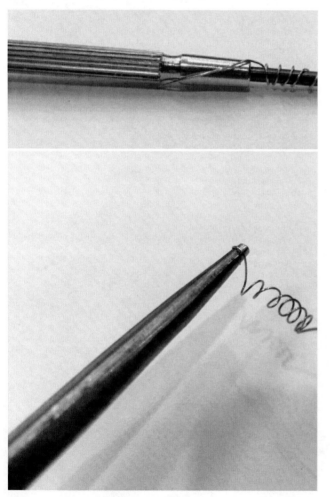

Here are a couple homemade tools using parts that were laying around the shop [or use your lathe]. Keep tension as you wind and make springs that look "factory"

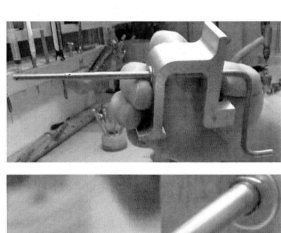

The epoxy tub repair kit does wonders. Black magic marker for numeral repair. You don't have to but, If you get micro-mesh sanding kit [grit sizes are like 1200, 1800, 2400, 3600, 4000, 8000 and 12,000] you can hide the patch well because the white tub acrylic is a perfect match. I have used them for years now. By the time you get to 12,000, its slick as glass.

Courtesy *David LaBounty*

Step two is to lower the profile of the screw head.

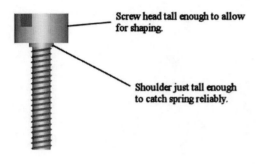

Screw head tall enough to allow for shaping.

Shoulder just tall enough to catch spring reliably.

Screw installed tight into arbor.

Peen end to secure screw.

File off the sides.

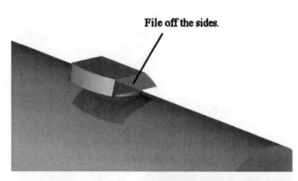

Round off head of the screw as the first step in shaping.

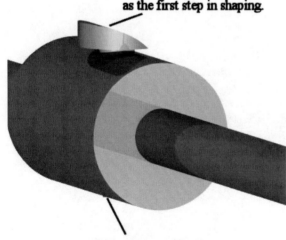

File peen down to arbor.

The final step is to round off the edges. Any sharp corners could damage the mainspring when fully wound.

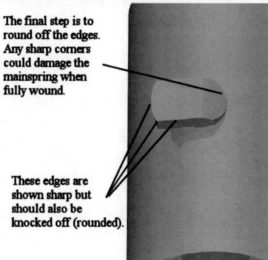

These edges are shown sharp but should also be knocked off (rounded).

Motion Work

Motion works

The term motion works refer to the additional gearing necessary to add a minute wheel/hand. The motion work is the small 12-to-1 reduction gear train that turns the timepiece's hour hand from the minute hand. It is attached to the going train by the friction coupling of the cannon pinion, so the minute and hour hands can be turned independently

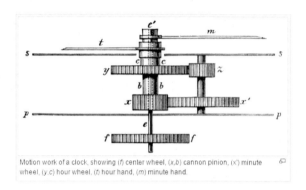

Motion work of a clock, showing (f) center wheel, (x,b) cannon pinion, (x') minute wheel, (y.c) hour wheel, (t) hour hand, (m) minute hand.

to set the timepiece. It is often located on the outside of the movement's front plate, just under the dial.

It consists of:

Cannon pinion- a pinion with a hollow shaft that fits friction tight over the center wheel shaft, projects through the clock face, and holds the minute hand. While the timepiece is not being set, this is turned by the center wheel and drives the minute wheel. While being set, it is turned by the setting mechanism, in modern clocks, a setting knob on the back of the clock. Setting the hands is done by opening the face and manually pushing the minute hand, which rotated the cannon pinion directly.

Minute wheel- It's pinion drives the hour wheel. During setting, this is driven by the intermediate wheel, and it turns both the

cannon pinion and the hour wheel, moving the hands.

Hour wheel- which fits over the shaft of the cannon pinion, and whose shaft holds the hour hand. The hour wheel rotates once for every 12 rotations of the cannon pinion/minute hand.

It would be possible to use only two wheels to make the gear reduction but that would leave the minute hand traveling counter clockwise. Not good.

ClickWork

The clickwork is a ratchet used so the user can wind up the clock spring without the arbor being able to spin backward. It consists of a gear, click and spring to keep the click engaged with the gear teeth. It is usually located outside the plates on the front side. It allows you to wind in one direction while keeping the mainspring from unwinding. This is because the click makes contact with the ratchet wheel and the ratchet wheel is affixed to the main wheel arbor. It is these clicks and click-springs that will allow you to "unwind" or take power off the mainspring.

The click holds back a lot of power. When you examine a movement while dismantled, test the click. It should rotate back and forth freely but not be loose. Make sure the spring is in good condition.

When oiling a movement, add a little oil to the click.

Make a dent with a center punch in the center of the top [big end] of the rivet. Drill the rivet out with a bit just larger than the hole in the wheel. Drill until you just reach the wheel, but do not cut the wheel. Now you can punch the remaining rivet out of the wheel, while supporting it on a staking block. Clean up the shape of the click with a file as necessary.

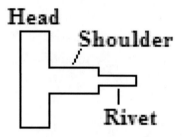

Make a new click rivet on the lathe. The click sits on the shoulder, which should be just a fraction bigger than the click so it will rotate smoothly. The rivet goes through the wheel or plate and is riveted over securely on the other side.

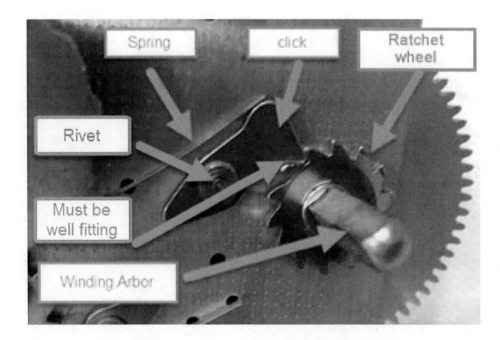

If the click is loose, it must be corrected for safety. It might be necessary to remove it and re-install it with a new rivet.

The mainspring provides the power to most old clocks, and this works very well. One problem older springs have is they tend to offer more power [torque] when fully wound, making the clock run faster, and less power when almost completely unwound, making the clock run slower.

A method of minimizing this uneven power is to use Stop Works. Stop Works comprises of two small wheels at the winding arbor. They restrict the winding to a specific number of winding turns, at the main part of the spring.

One of the wheels, called the star wheel, has an odd number of teeth and has one tooth valley that is not as deep as the rest. The other wheel called the finger wheel has an even number of teeth, and one tooth is longer than the rest. This combination, when set up correctly, restricts the number of turns and thus the clock power, to the middle portion of the mainspring, providing a more even distribution of power.

Another method, known as The Geneva Stop Work, also known as the Maltese Cross, uses different shaped wheels. The convex portion stops any further rotation beyond the designed number of turns. Four in this case.

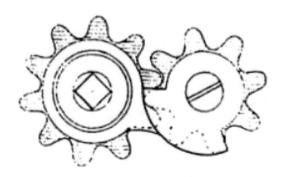

While the movement is dismantled, we need to carefully examine the mainspring to ensure it has not lost its power or, worse still broken. At best, we need to grease the spring before putting it back into the movement.

To examine the spring properly, we must first uncoil it and remove it from its wheel. To do this, we can use an inexpensive mainspring winder [about $10]. Using this winder, we can release the power under control. You must use a thick glove when using this tool to protect your hand and use eye protection.

The winder, is placed over the spring, with the post [right side of the photo below], placed through the loop of the spring. The clamp [left side] is tightened onto the edge of the wheel.

Holding the spring with the gloved hand, you can wind up the mainspring enough to remove the C-clamp or wire, release the click and let down the power using a let-down key.

If you don't keep tight hold, the spring can get away from you. Springs can have a mind of their own sometimes. Don't ask how I know.

Once the spring has been let down, make a note of the orientation of the spring on the arbor on your notes, and remove the arbor from the spring. It might need to be coaxed off using the genital force of a small screwdriver. Remove the winder and set the spring on the table.

The spring uncoiled or relaxed should be at least three times bigger than when it is fully wound. If it is not, it is "set" or lost its power and needs to be replaced.

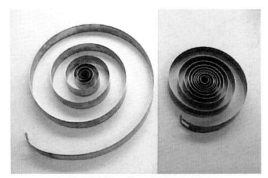

The spring on the left is new.
The one on the right is old and "set."

To order a new spring, you need to measure the width [½", ¾" etc], thickness [0.013", 0.018" etc], and its length in inches. Then go to the mainspring chart from your parts supplier's catalog. The strength is the thickness of the mainspring, and the length is the complete length of the uncoiled mainspring. To measure the length, clamp the outer end in a vice and stretch out the spring until only two or three inner coils remain. Measure this length and guess the extra amount left in the last coils.

Note: new mainsprings, as supplied, are coated with a rust inhibitor rather than a lubricant, and they need to be cleaned and lubricated before being put into the movement.

If you are interested, the Mainspring Length Formula is:

$$L_{MS} = \frac{1}{2 \times T_{MS}} \times \left[\frac{(\pi \times D_B^2)}{4} - \frac{(\pi \times D_A^2)}{4} \right]$$

where,
L_{MS} is the mainspring length
T_{MS} is the mainspring thickness
D_B is the inside diameter of the barrel
D_A is the outside diameter of the barrel arbor

If the original spring is not broken or set, you can clean the spring and grease it up. Clean it in the regular cleaning solution and dry it thoroughly.

The method I use is the simplest and easiest I know of. It involves a little stretching and no special setup.

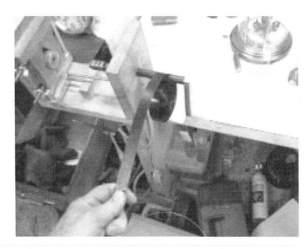

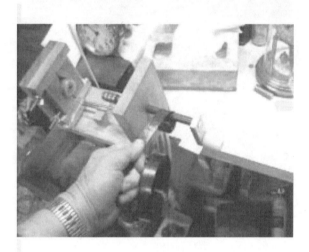

mainspring lube, and lubricate it all the way up, and back again.

I have used 90W, EP gear oil on mainsprings for many years with excellent results. 90W means 90 Weight, and EP means Extreme Pressure. It is commonly available anywhere automotive oils are sold. I use it because I wound numerous mainsprings in a mainspring winder after they were lubricated, and watched the springs uncoil as I slowly unwound them. I concluded that springs with this oil expanded more evenly than ones lubricated with most mainspring greases, particularly within their working range.

Reattach the arbor to the spring. If the spring was hard to remove from the arbor, it might need adjusting before it can be reattached. The innermost coil of the spring must match the same diameter as the arbor, or the notch on the arbor will not re-engage with the spring hole. If necessary, make the inner coil smaller using smooth jawed needle-nose pliers.

With the spring unwound, I hook it over the handle of a winder, between the coils, not through the center. A screwdriver clamped in a bench vise will do as well. Move up a few inches at a time, letting it coil back up below, until I get to the center, then releasing it a few inches at a time so it can coil back up normally. I don't try to mess with those last few tight coils in the center, which don't do anything anyway. But I do check for cracks or tears in the arbor-hook hole or nearby.

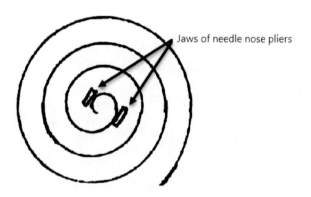

Jaws of needle nose pliers

Pulling it through, I scrub it down the full length with steel wool dipped in mineral spirits, removing rust and crud and inspecting for cracks and problem areas. I wipe it down the entire length with a rag as I let it coil back up. Then I take a cloth charged with

If your mainspring is contained in a barrel,

you can remove it with the Ollie Baker [or similar] winder, or by carefully pulling the center coil out and peeling it out of the barrel. Before taking the cover off, mark the barrel where the cover notch is located so it can go back on in the same location. Also, mark the cover and barrel with an S for strike or T for time so they go back the same way they came off.

Be careful. You don't want to bend the innermost coil of the mainspring any more than you have to.

Test wind and unwind the spring at least a couple of times after you've reassembled the mainspring/great wheel assembly. It's also a good idea to gently try to pull the arbor out of the inner coil to make sure it won't release easily. It's frustrating to get everything back together again only to find out that your spring isn't catching anymore. Once it is caught, wind it up tight, and the inner coil will be forced around the arbor, conforming it to the proper shape.

Use the mainspring winder to put the C-clamp back on.

Remove the barrel cover by rapping the arbor on a piece of wood. The cover will pop off. Grasp the two inner coils [the ones closest to the center] with a pair of smooth-faced pliers and gently pull the coils out until they are "free" of the barrel. Then slowly and steadily pull the "exposed" coils, by hand, until the mainspring starts to come out.

When several coils are "exposed", grasp the coils with a gloved hand and "guide" the rest of the mainspring out of the barrel. What I mean by guiding is NOT pulling on the spring but a sort of twist and tug which will loosen the coils and the mainspring will almost come out on its own. Please be CAREFUL. This is something that you must "feel" as you go, and it takes some practice. Make a note of the orientation of the arbor on your notes and remove the arbor from the spring.

The $10 mainspring winder mentioned above is not ideal for dealing with powerful mainsprings, as, it will only work on loop end mainsprings. A better solution is the full-on mainspring winder.

I believe the best winder is the Ollie Baker style mainspring winder. It handles loop-end and hole-end springs, as well as springs in a barrel, safely. It utilizes a full set of sturdy sleeves to fit all sizes of springs. Use it with your let down keys and spring clamps.

Holding a barrel using the hose clamp

Homemade mainspring winder

"Turns of Power"

Plans for the Joe Collins Mainspring Winder follow.

Count, or calculate, how many turns of the mainwheel your clock will need to run for eight days. On many German clocks, the time side will need around 4, 360 degree turns [often a little less for the strike side]. So, you need good power for that number of turns   [A].

Next, from the fully let down position, start to wind up the mainspring until the point where the spring makes a shuffling noise in its barrel. Now, from that point, carefully count how many full 360 degree turns it takes to wind the spring entirely up. This gives you the "turns of power" that your spring can provide [B].

If [B] is greater than [A], you're good to go ...

On an open spring, you count the number of 360 degree turns while carefully letting the fully wound Main Spring down until the spring barely touches a stop post or the 2nd wheel pinion. This gives you the turns of available power [B].

Note, round off any fractional turn to the closest 1/2 turn.

When the mainspring has been cleaned, examined, lubricated and is ready to return to the movement, put it on the mainspring winder and wind it up tight. Wipe off any excess lubrication and let the spring entirely down again. Do this several times to distribute the lubrication evenly on the entire spring before finally installing the C clamp or barrel, ready to install in the movement. This practice will also test the spring has no weaknesses that likely to fail soon after installation.

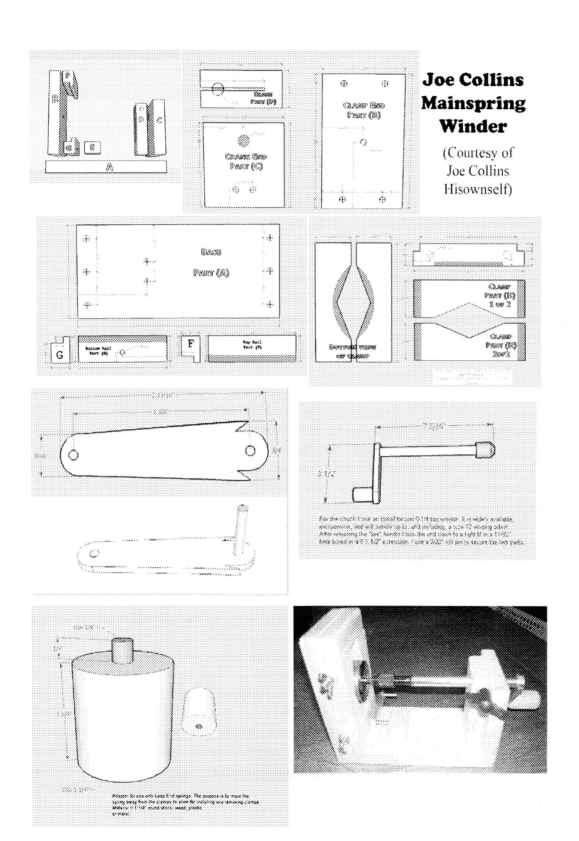

Joe Collins Mainspring Winder

(Courtesy of Joe Collins Hisownself)

Reassembly

When the pivots are smooth and the pivot holes are all correct, insert each wheel in place **by itself** between the plates and make sure it spins freely, smoothly and with a little endshake. Test the spin in several positions, top plate up, top plate down, escape wheel up, escape wheel down, looking for any possible interference. It should come to a very gradual stop, not a sudden halt. Rotating the plates up and down, the wheel should drop onto the other shoulder freely.

When all have been tested individually, insert two at a time to test the mesh of each wheel and pinion teeth. Use only light pressure to feel any roughness in the mesh at any point. Then turn them fast to observe them coming to a very gradual stop. When each pair has been tested, insert all the wheels in the **time train only,** not including the escapement. Test that they all spin freely, the teeth mesh correctly and they come to a very gradual stop.

Look for any wobble in any wheel. Do the same for the striking train and chime train if the movement has one. **If you skip this procedure, you will likely regret it later.**

Next, do a final cleaning in a fresh solution. Then insert everything back into the plates using gloves without touching the parts with your bare hands. Or use disposable finger cots.

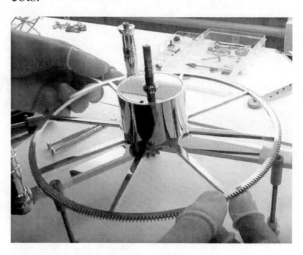

Place the plate that contains the pillars on your box or movement pillars. Refer to your photos, diagrams, and notes. Reset all the wheels and levers in place.

It is often most efficient to insert the wheels into the bottom plate in this order: Center wheel, third wheel, two great wheels, hammer, pinwheel, escape wheel, gathering-pallet wheel, warning wheel, and lastly, the fly.

Bring the second plate down. One by one using tweezers, locate the top pivots back into their pivot holes. Do not use pliers or anything stronger than tweezers. The pivots can bend or even broken off very easily.

You will find each arbor is a slightly different length. Knowing this, look for the tallest and fit that first, then move on down until you get the shortest. You can add a couple of rubber bands around the front and back plates to hold it all together until everything is in the correct location.

Typically, the great wheel [home to the mainspring] is tallest with its winding arbor. Once this is in place, you can usually start a turn of the nuts on the two bottom pillars, then work up the train until you can start a turn on the other two pillar nuts. Each wheel will click in place, which I find very satisfying. When the last pivot is located, the upper plate will come down onto the shoulders of the pillars.

This can be a tricky process at first, but it soon becomes easier once you have done it several times, and you are more familiar with the parts. Be patient and be prepared that you might have to take the movement apart again and start over if fine-tuning is needed. Never force anything and take your time. Make it a habit of testing everything you add during assembly to catch any faults before you get too far. To verify a wheel is in its correct place, using tweezers, slide the arbor up and down. If it is in place, it will slide up and down freely. If it is frozen in place, it is trapped between the plates, not in its pivot holes.

For movements with a striking train, first, when you assemble the clock, make sure that the maintenance wheel is adjusted so that the count lever is in a deep notch and the maintenance lever is at the bottom of the maintenance cam. That takes care of [1] and [2]. Then, try to adjust the warning wheel so that the warning pin is about 1/2 turn away from the locking lever. The reason is that the warning wheel is spinning very fast, so it needs some "lead distance" to make sure the locking lever is down before the warning pin gets to it. [See the striking section later in this book for more information on this setup]

When you are satisfied it is all correct, tighten the movement nuts or taper pins, and wind the spring a little to remove the mainspring clamps. I recommend you use a brass pin in a steel pillar, to prevent the pin from getting stuck in a steel mating hole over time.

Occasionally you will find that once a wheel is in place and the levers fitted [especially with rack and snail] you can't access the oil sink. In that case, it is best to oil that pivot during assembly.

Striking Setup

It is essential to have a good understanding of the correct striking set up when you put a time and strike movement back together.

After all the wheels are set between the plates, some adjustments are usually necessary for the striking to work correctly and in sync. This explanation is for the more common Count Wheel striking system only.

It's Operation

The count wheel system uses a large extra wheel on or driven by the winding arbor on the strike train. The count wheel has a series of regular teeth and some extra deep slot teeth. The deep slot allows the count lever to drop deeper at the end of the striking sequence. At one o'clock, there are two deep slots next to each other, so the clock strikes once and stops. At two o'clock, there is a shallow slot and then a deep slot. This allows the clock to strike twice before stopping. Etc. The speed of the train and thus the striking is controlled by a fly which acts as an airbrake to slow the strike train and ensure a measured beat. There are usually two combination

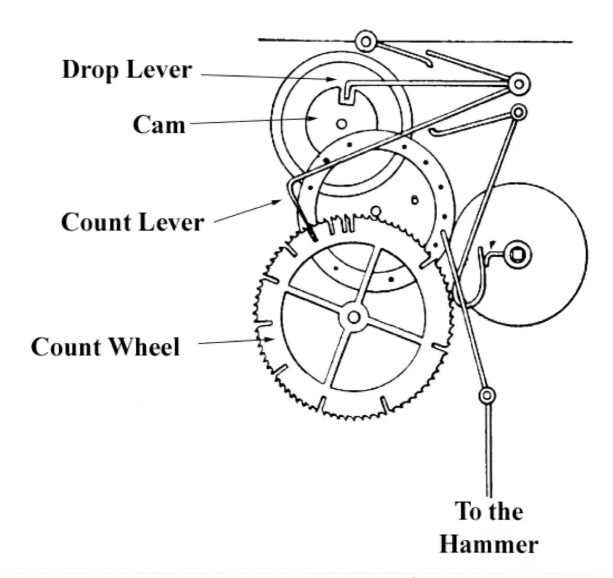

Drop Lever

Cam

Count Lever

Count Wheel

To the Hammer

167 | Page The Grandfather Clock Owner's Repair Manual

levers. One raises the other, and both combine to set up the warning run, hold it until the proper time, release it, and then count the strikes.

First, make sure the **Count Lever** points directly to the center of the count wheel. Adjust it if necessary.

These three items must all be correct at the same time:

- Count Lever in a deep slot.
- Drop Lever must sit in the slot of the Cam.
- Locking Lever must be engaged with the Lock Pin.

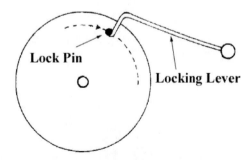

If the Locking Lever is not sitting next to the Lock Pin, you may need to open the movement and adjust the meshing of the teeth, so it does sit next to the Lock Pin, while the Count Lever is still in a deep slot **and** the Drop Lever is still in the Cam slot.

You only want to advance the wheel that is in the incorrect position [usually the locking pin wheel], leaving the rest in the same location. This is easier said than done. To help, press a small amount of Rodico into the wheels you want to stay the same, allowing you to focus on the incorrect wheel. Capture the mainspring before making any adjustments.

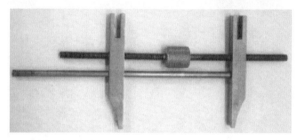

A plate spreader is a very useful tool. It allows you to spread the plates just enough to make minor gear meshing adjustments without dismantling the whole movement or disturbing the other wheels in the train.

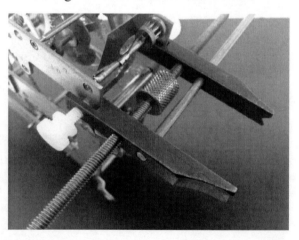

Test it over at least a 24-hour period to make sure everything is working correctly.

in such a manner that the lifter falls exactly when the minute hand is upright [exactly at 12]. Put the minute hand on the square of the cannon pinion and see that it does so, or move the cannon pinion a few teeth in the minute wheel until right.

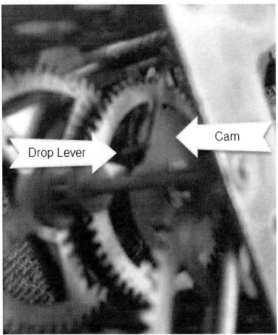

When assembling the movement, the cannon pinion and minute wheel must work together

A- Stop Lever

B- Maintenance Lever

C- Count Lever

D- Lift Lever

E- Warning Lever

F- "J" Lever

G- Hammer Lever

H- Stop/Warning Wheel

I- Maintenance Cam

J- 2nd Wheel

K- Count Wheel

L- Strike Release Pins

M- Hammer Detent

N- Hammer

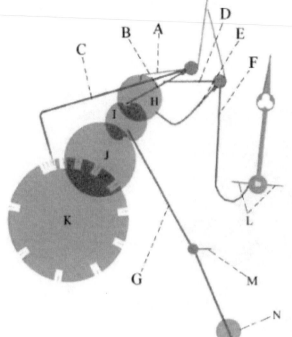

Before you dismantle the movement, look carefully at the set-up. You will likely see three sets of levers. Each set is attached to an arbor between the plates.

- Upper Lifting levers
- Lower Lifting levers
- Hammer levers

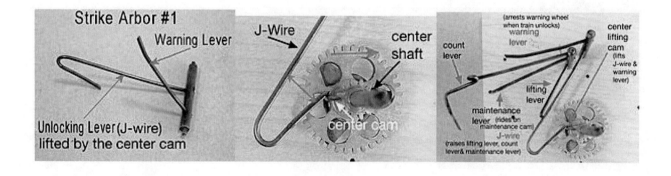

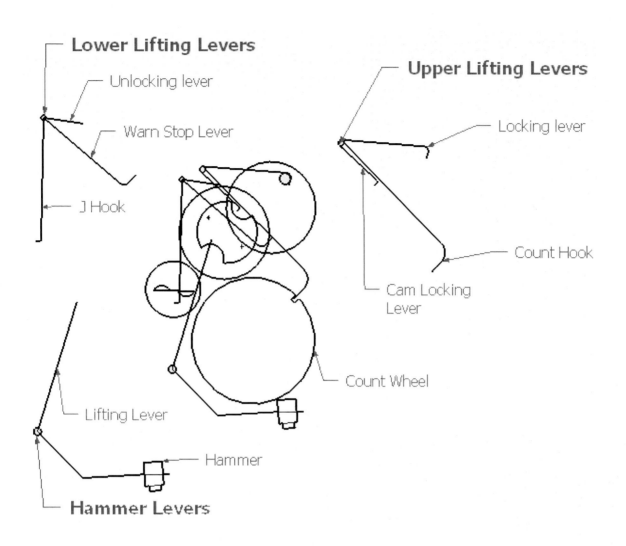

Lower Lifting Levers

Unlocking lever

Warn Stop Lever

J Hook

Upper Lifting Levers

Locking lever

Count Hook

Cam Locking Lever

Count Wheel

Lifting Lever

Hammer

Hammer Levers

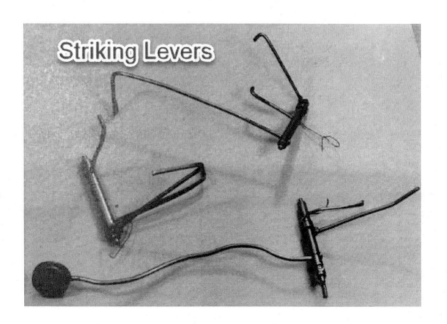

Striking Levers

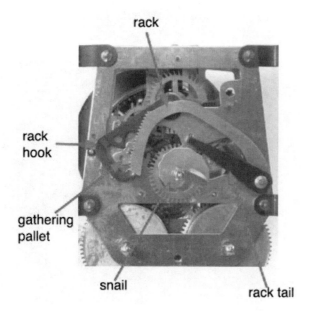

rack

rack hook

gathering pallet

snail

rack tail

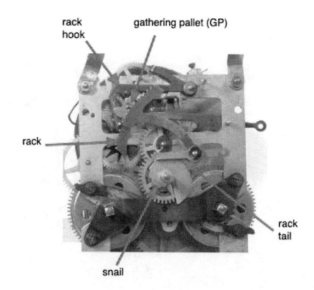

rack hook

gathering pallet (GP)

rack

rack tail

snail

These are two common examples of Rack & Snail striking movements. This is a modern upgrade from the older more primitive count wheel system which is prone to getting out of sync.

The main mechanical components of every rack-striking clock are:

- saw-toothed rack, with a tail
- nautilus-shaped snail, with 12 steps that turn with the hour hand.
- rack hook, to support the rack
- gathering pallet, to engage the teeth of the rack

The snail, with its ever-enlarging radius, determines the number to strike and is indexed by the rack tail. The rack counts off the strike.

- When the rack hook is fully dropped beneath the rack,
- The warning pin is resting against the locking stub; and
- The projection on the rack hook is nestled in the dent of the bean cam.

That means the rack hook is synchronized with the warning wheel.

The cam is a pressed fit on its arbor. It can be adjusted either by twisting it on the arbor or by prying it off and repositioning it with its recess against the rack hook pin. Do this while the warning pin is against the locking flag. Observe the position of the pinwheel. There should be a little run before the next pin lifts the hammer.

Identify these parts. Each Rack and Snail striking movement will have some variation on this concept.

The Lift Cam on the minute arbor lifts the Hour Warning Lever.

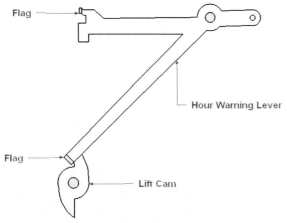

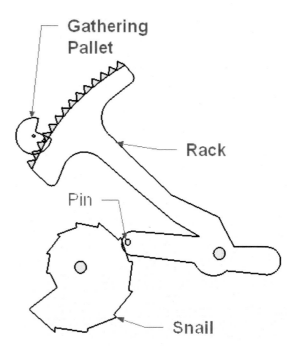

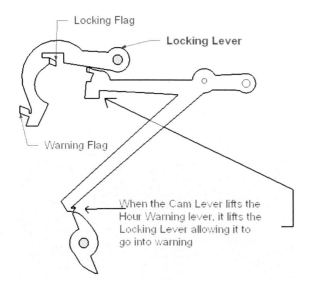

When it goes into warning, the pin on the Rack lands on the Snail to determine how many times to strike. The Gathering Pallet advances the Rack until the correct number of bell or gong strikes have sounded.

The advantage Rack & Snail has over the Count Wheel system is the striking stays synchronized with the hour hand, so it always strikes the correct hour. The Count Wheel will get out of sync if the hands are advanced without allowing the strike [and Count Wheel] to stay synchronized.

Chiming Setup
My favorite method is to take the chime count wheel off and let the chime run until it stops. That will be the auto synch position. Put the wheel back on at the 3/4 hour position and turn the chime drum at the back until you get the four or eight-note descending scale that is both the 1/4 hour and the end of the 3/4 hour chime. That will get everything working together correctly.

Replacing the Hammer Leather

Cut the leather, enough to fold over.

Soak it in water with some PVA glue [Elmers-Glue] in it.

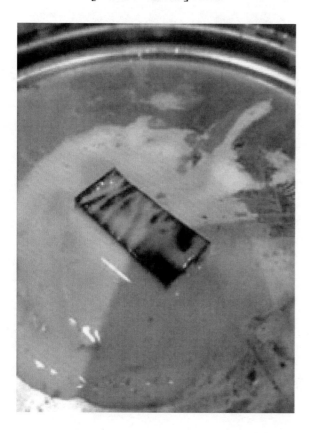

Fold it over, shape it in a split stake, and close it up in a vice.

Take it out when dried up.

Cut to length, glues it in, and shape the end with sandpaper.

Congratulations, you are now **hooked.**

Lubricating the Movement

Lubricants provide a protective film that separates the two rubbing surfaces and reduces the level of friction in the two rubbing surfaces. The correct oiling of the movement is critical. There are many specialty clock oils available which you can use, but there is an ideal motor oil. Mobil 1 Synthetic– 0W-40 for pivots and Mobil 1 Synthetic 10W-60 for mainsprings. Having used this for years, I have found it does not go gummy, is not too thin to run out and is compatible with the typical clock metals.

A fellow clock repairer used to be a chemist and studied the various clock oils on the market and their viscosity, and recommended Mobile 1 to me.

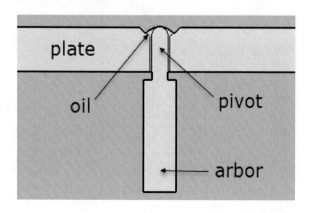

Insert only a small amount of oil in the oil sink. Oil is held in place by capillary attraction and surface tension. If you insert too much oil, the oil will be drawn out and leave it dry. No more oil should be used than is needed to coat the pivot and pivot hole.

Ideally, use a heavy lubricant for high-torque, low-speed applications [mainspring, 1st and 2nd wheel pivots] like Mobile-1 10W-40. Use a light lubricant for low-torque, high-speed applications [3rd, 4th, escape wheel pivots, balance pivots, escape wheel teeth, clock strike governor pivots, etc.] like Mobile-1 0W-40.

Approximate Viscosities of Common Materials	
Material	Viscosity in Centipoise @70F
Water	1
Milk	3
Nye Clock Oil 140B	20
Sperm Oil	52
SAE 10 Motor Oil	85-140
SAE 20 Motor Oil	140-420
SAE 30 Motor Oil	420-650
SAE 40 Motor Oil	650-900
Mobil 1 5W-30	178
Mobil 1 0W-40	215
Mobil 1 5W-40	250
Mobil 1 10W-40	325
SAE 80W-90	585
SAE 85W140	1750

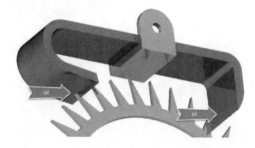

Place one drop of oil on the escapement pallet impulse faces. Do not oil any of the wheel teeth.

Place one drop on each lever post, the minute wheel post, the escapement post and on each click.

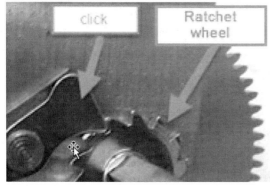

click   Ratchet wheel

Test Run

The test stand below fits many movements just sitting on top. It is easy to make using ½" plywood. 12" tall, 8" wide and 6" deep. Cut a hole in the top about 4" by 3" or to suit your movement. The pendulum [and weight chains if it has weights] fit through the hole in the top. Make a second top out of ¼" ply to fit smaller movements. An added front piece will accept movements screwed to its face. Cut a hole in it if needed.

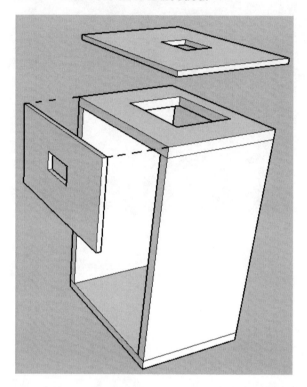

Screw the movement to a [homemade] test stand, clamped to a benchtop or table. Make sure it is level to the eye. Add the pendulum, wind it up and start the clock to make sure it runs. Closely observe the movement and listen to all sounds. The tick and tock should be even. Adjust the pendulum crutch if it is not even. Adjust its regulation until it keeps good time.

When I say level, I find my students get paranoid about 'level.' The fact is the movement needs to be placed on the stand so it is 'in beat' [see the first chapter]. There is no guarantee the movement will be set in the case perfectly level, and the place the clock sets might not be perfectly level.

Make sure it runs for a full 24 hours before putting the movement back into its case.

For clocks with weights, if you have a table that takes leaves? Open it just a crack for the chains, hang the weights under the table, and voila! Instant workbench I did that a few times when I was first starting out.

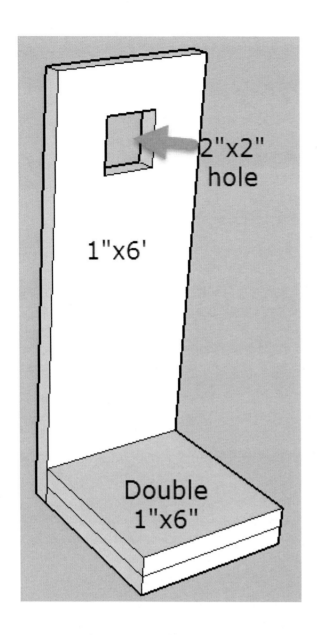

2"x2" hole

1"x6'

Double 1"x6"

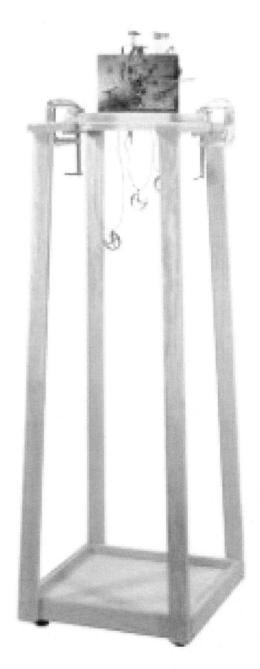

If you are working on a Grandfather Clock [Correctly called a Longcase clock in the UK and Tall case Clock in the US], a taller stand is needed, giving room for the long pendulum to swing, and the weights room to drop.

Five feet tall is a good height. That is plenty of room for the pendulum and for the weights to run the clock for several days, and the movement will be at eye level.

Or, you can create a wall shelf to test these movements.

After Servicing Troubleshooting

In a perfect world, after you have finished servicing your clock movement, it would run perfectly the first time. However, we all know this is not a perfect world. If you put your serviced movement on the test stand and it will not run, follow this process.

Assuming it runs but slows down and stops, look to see if the escapement is caught on a tooth, or swinging free of either pallet. If it is caught on a pallet/tooth, it is most likely an imperfect tooth, or the escapement needs adjusting. See above.

If it is free of the tooth, it is not getting enough power. Your work needs checking.

Try removing all but the last two wheels on the time side – i.e., the escape wheel and the next wheel down the chain. Add the escapement and hang a weight from the wheel before the escape wheel. Make sure it is pulling in the power direction. If it does not run, the problem is right there. If it does run, add one more wheel and test again with the weight on the lowest wheel. Keep testing until it refuses to run.

The wire to the pendulum rod must be close-fitting in the crutch fork. If it is loose, it will lose energy jumping the gap from one side to the other. Close the gap, so it is almost but not quite touching each side of the loop.

You may find a small notch, or at least a rough place, worn there. Dress it out perfectly smooth, or your clock will likely not work well. Small as it may seem, it stops many clocks.

Make sure the wire in this area is clean and bright and, to avoid any energy loss in the touching surfaces and provide a little oil.

High-Speed Test

One test I use quite often is a high-speed test. It is simple, lubricate up all pivots, remove the escapement lever and let the movement spin. Listen, and it should produce an even whirr sound. No pops and crackle noise. Watch the speed consistency, and any irregularities will show in unison with a particular gear rotation.

The high-speed test is useful for spotting train problems, especially in the slower gears. This test with the low-speed test [low inertia -couple clicks on mainspring or small weight and freewheeling no escapement] is a good combo diagnostic.

When doing the test, mark any suspect gear when the train stops and retest to see if the same location reappears. The idea is that low power can't overcome the problem area and becomes a pointer to the problem tooth, etc..

The high-speed test is also good for revealing bent arbor/pivot as tone/speed changes with cycling of the problem gear. The smallest arbor pivot bend is magnified and revealed by sound.

A perfect train should have an even whirr. Pops are quite often bad trundles/ pinions.

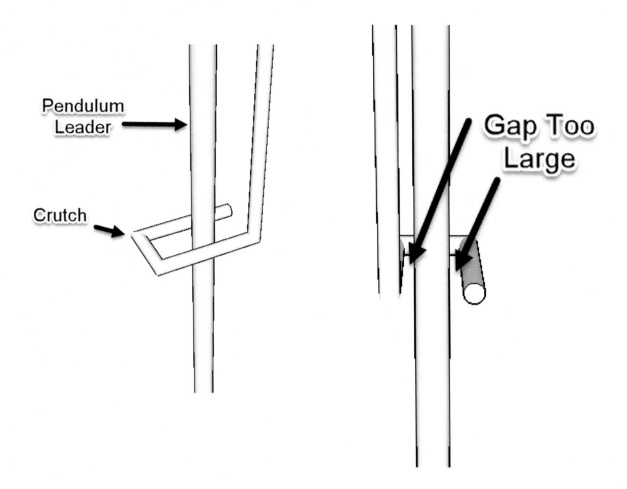

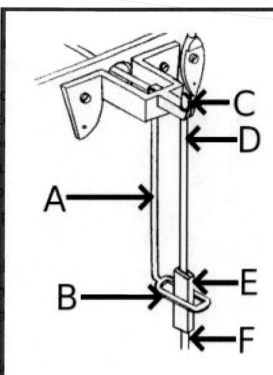

A: Crutch Arm B:
Crutch Fork C: Top
Suspension Block D:
Suspension Spring E:
Lower Suspension
Block F: Pendulum
Rod

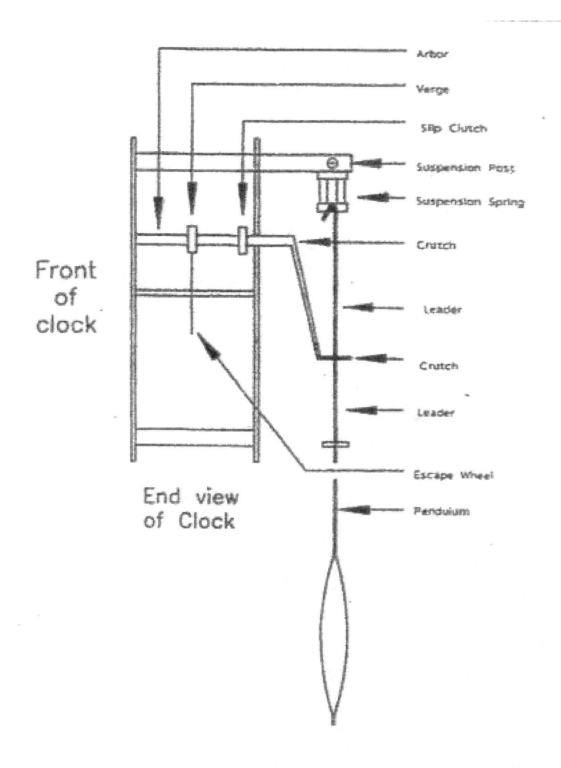

Front
of
clock

End view
of Clock

Arbor

Verge

Slip Clutch

Suspension Post

Suspension Spring

Crutch

Leader

Crutch

Leader

Escape Wheel

Pendulum

The 'cock' that supports the escapement is often friction fitted to the plate. The position of the escapement can be adjusted up or down with pliers [closer or further from the escape wheel]. Make tiny adjustments only if you are sure it is needed.

Put the Movement back in the Case

Only after you have tested the movement, made any adjustments, and tested it again for several days, you can then put the movement back in its case. Use the same screws that came out.

Reaching down into the case can be tricky, if not impossible, without the use of a slotted [not Philips] "screw holding screwdriver." They are available at many good hardware stores or online. A flashlight is helpful also.

Timesavers sells a 10" Screw-Holding Screwdriver #13552 for $12.

Phillips screws were not used in the old clock, and I recommend you do not use Philips screws if replacements screws are needed. Do not be tempted to use a magnetic screwdriver. Magnetism can affect the operation of a clock, so it is normal to have a 'de-magnetizer' handy on the clock bench.

Timesavers #:*23461* $4

When installing the hands, it is very important they fit snugly so the stay in the correct alignment. If they are loose, one hand might start to catch on the other hand, the dial or the glass, which will likely stop the clock.

Make sure the minute hand is not too close to the hour hand at the arbor. This can also stop the clock and be hard to diagnose.

Install the Hands

First, put the minute hand on and adjust it forward to point precisely to 12. It usually has a square hole that fits on the square shaft. Remove the minute hand again for a moment.

Now, the hour hand is installed. It is usually friction fit onto the hour pipe. Set it to point precisely to the 12.

Next, reinstall the minute hand to the 12 o'clock position again. Both should now point precisely to the 12 at the same time. The clock is now correctly set.

If the movement includes a striking train, advance the minute hand until the clock strikes. Count the number of strikes and make the necessary adjustments to the hands. Repeat this several times to make sure it is correct.

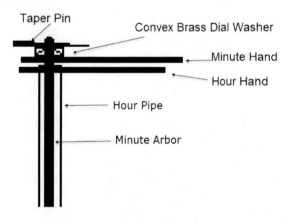

As you will note, the minute hand is very close to the hour hand, and the hour hand is very close to the clock dial. For this reason, the hands must be held firmly in place, so nothing touches each other. If the hands touch each other, the clock will stop.

The minute hand is held in place using a Convex Brass Dial Washer and either a taper pin or nut. Install a suitable dial washer, so the minute hand is held tight when the pin or nut is snugged up.

Above is an assortment of dial washers.

If you lose or break the hands, replacements are available. The length of the minute hand should just reach the chapter ring and the hour hand point to the numbers.

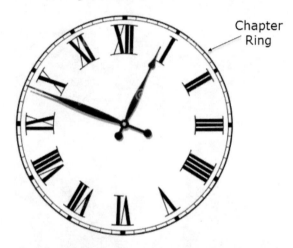

New taper pins are available at the parts houses or you can make your own in a minute or two if you own a lathe.

Be sure to trim the pin to a suitable length for a tidy finish.

The Work Area

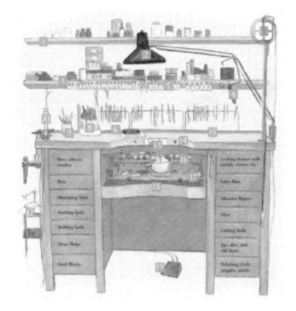

The worktop needs to be about 30" above the floor and well lit. In front of a window is nice, a fluorescent light is good, giving nice even light. Two folding desk lights are also good, providing light from two directions.

It is essential the floor be clean and tidy and preferably not carpet. It won't be long before you drop a small part on the floor and it needs to be easy to find. Some people create a pull-out screen that comes out from the worktop to catch small items.

It is best if pets, especially cats, cannot roam on your work area that can knock things over or small children with curious fingers.

The most important thing is, all your tools be within reach.

A well-designed clock shop is a tool in itself.

Having everything to hand, everything in its place, space to work on clocks is an asset, a place you want to be.

Working on clocks does not require a lot of space, at least at first. You need a clean and clear work surface about 24" by 24" to work on the clock. You also need an area for cleaning parts, a place for your lathe of whatever type nearby, and a space to run the clock while testing.

You can start by working on your kitchen table, but as you get more serious, you will want a dedicated space. A roll-top desk or an old office desk works well.

Going Electronic

If we want to get more technical about correctly setting up the beat of a clock, or diagnosing problems, we can introduce some electronic assistance.

The first item is a beat amplifier, available from Timesavers or Radio Shack for under $20, or your clock supply house. Using an alligator clip, attach the amplifier to the mechanism plate and turn it on. It will amplify the tick-tock sound making it much easier to get the beat accurately adjusted.

MicroSet

To get more technical, there is the MicroSet, which is a digital electronic timer.

It provides unprecedented accuracy, a resolution to a millionth of a second, an optical sensor to eliminate false readings from extraneous noise, and a powerful interface to Macintosh and Windows personal computers. The Count Mode will find the correct rate of any running pendulum clock. The Strike Mode will record the pattern of strikes over many hours to find intermittent problems. There are also several optional features that can be added.

With this information, you can identify defective escape wheel teeth and put a clock

in beat very precisely by reading the digital display.

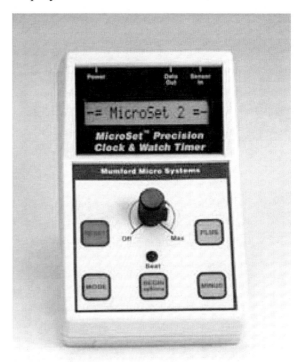

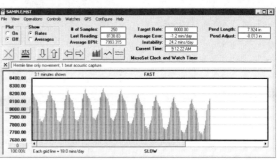

Refinishing the Clock Case

Many of the clock cases you come across are very dirty, often very dark from the years of household furniture polish and normal dust floating in the air and probably smoke. The motto "Do No Harm" means we want to restore the clock back to its original state as close as possible while doing as little damage or alteration as possible.

Start by taking the case apart as much as you can: movement, glass, hardware. Our goal is to remove the dirt and furniture polish back to the original French polish finish underneath.

There are many cleaning products on the market that will remove the dirt. However, most of these products will work too well and damage the original polish below over time. We learn from museum restoration practices that any cleaner with a PH above 7.0 will not only clean as you work on the clock but will continue to eat at the surface long after you have finished, damaging the original polish or shellac.

My recommendation is to use "Mr. Clean." This product happens to have the perfect PH value at just under 7.0 and removes the dirt with minimal effort. Just put some Mr. Clean on #0000 Steel Wood and using light pressure in a circular motion, clean off the dirt. You will likely see the hidden wood grain re-appear.

At this point, using a soft cotton rag and giving a little pressure to rub the surface and generate a little heat to reactivate the shellac. If the original surface has minor damage like scratches, watermarks, or 'alligatoring' [a series of cracks grouped in one area], you can use an "Amalgamator" from Mohawk. Used carefully, it will reactivate the shellac a little and blend it to create a newly restored finish.

Any loose veneer can be reglued using "Hide Glue." This is the type of glue used by the original case maker, and we still use the modern version from Titebond because it can be unglued using vinegar, and re-glued after repairs and restoration had been completed.

Once all the dirt is removed, you need to "feed" the wood again. For this, it is recommended you use Howard "Feed-n-Wax" orange oil, which is readily available. This will stop the pores from completely drying out and give life back to the wood.

The final step is to protect the clock case with Bri-Wax to give a mat shine that resembles the original hand rubbed French Polish.

If the original finish is too severely damaged, use a good quality stripper to remove the old finish. Do not use a water-based stripper or it will likely harm the veneer. Make sure 100% of the old finish is removed. Use gloves and eye protection. Let the stripper sit for at least 15 if not 30 minutes to allow it time to do its work. Repeat the stripper if necessary.

When all the finish is off, wash the case with mineral spirits to remove any residue.

Sand all the bare wood, starting with 300 grit, working up to 800 grit. Wipe clean with a tack cloth.

Staining the case is optional. Some feel it enhances the natural wood grain. I like Minwax. After staining, use #0000 steel wool and wipe clean with an old t-shirt.

Others prefer to see the woods natural color without stain.

Next, use a wood filler. Not to fill holes but to fill the wood pores. Wipe on, leave for 15 minutes and buff off with burlap.

Lastly, add a seal coat. Varnish is suitable but takes days to dry and picks up any dust in the air. Do not use Polyurethane.

The best choice is Tung Oil. Plan on 6 to 10 coats, letting each coat dry overnight and rubbing with #0000 steel wool and a t-shirt before applying the next coat. You will be delighted with the finish, and it is foolproof.

The very first clock ever made, several hundred years ago, was a revolution, as before them time was relative to the sun up and sundown. When mechanical clocks were first invented, they changed everything.

The first clocks only ran for a few hours and needed winding every day.

The next generation of clocks used gearing to run for a week without winding. This was much more convenient.

Following this, newer clocks could run for a full month without winding, but these were only made for the very wealthy.

In 1841, the 400 Day Clock, with its unique torsion pendulum, was first invented and patented by American Aaron Crane. The term "Anniversary clock" was copyrighted by Bowler & Burdock Company in 1901, an Ohio clock-making firm. It ran for well over one year.

An Anniversary clock or 400-day clock is called a torsion pendulum clock. It is a mechanical clock that keeps time with a mechanism called a torsion pendulum. This is a weighted disk or wheel, often a decorative wheel with 3 or 4 chrome balls on ornate spokes, suspended by a thin wire or ribbon called a torsion spring [also known as "suspension spring"].

The torsion pendulum rotates about the vertical axis, twisting it, instead of swinging like an ordinary pendulum. The force of the twisting torsion spring reverses the direction of rotation, so the torsion pendulum oscillates slowly, clockwise and then counterclockwise.

The clock's gears apply a pulse of torque to the top of the torsion spring with each rotation, to keep the wheel going. The torsion spring functions similarly to a watch's hairspring, as a harmonic oscillator to control the rate of the clock's hands. In 1951, Charles Terwilliger of the Horolovar Co. invented a temperature compensating suspension spring, which allowed fairly accurate clocks to be made.

Description

Torsion clocks are usually delicate, spring-wound clocks. The polished clock mechanism is exposed under a glass case or dome, to allow people to watch the torsion pendulum turn. It can also be in the form of a lantern.

Known as 400-day or Anniversary clocks, because they can run for more than a year on a single winding. This does not mean they will keep accurate time the whole year. For more precise timekeeping, it's best to wind the clock once a month. Some models will even run up to 1000 days on a single winding.

Mechanism

Torsion clocks are capable of running much longer between windings than clocks with an ordinary pendulum because the torsion pendulum rotates slowly and takes very little energy. They are challenging to set up and are usually not as accurate as clocks with an ordinary pendulum. One reason, changes in temperature due to the elasticity of the spring.

The rate of the clock can be made faster or slower by an adjustment screw mechanism on the torsion pendulum that moves the weight balls in or out from the axis. The closer in the balls are, the smaller the moment of inertia of the torsion pendulum, and the faster it will turn.

One oscillation of the torsion pendulum usually takes 12, 15, or 20 seconds. A crutch device at the top of the torsion spring engages a lever with two anchor-shaped arms; the arms in turn alternately engage the teeth of the escape wheel. As the anchor releases a tooth of the escape wheel, the lever, which is fixed to the anchor, moves to one side and, via the crutch, gives a small twist to the top of the torsion spring. This is just enough to perpetuate the oscillation.

The Atmos clock, made by Jaeger Le Coultre, is a type of torsion clock that doesn't need to be wound or powered at all. The mainspring which turns the clock's wheels is kept wound by small changes in atmospheric pressure and/or local temperature, using a bellows mechanism. Thus no winding key or battery is needed, and it can run for years without human intervention.

The Anniversary clock is, to some degree, a different animal, but in many respects, they are straightforward to service. They are simple in the respect that they are time only, with no striking or chiming trains, no levers, and pins.

Movements come in four basic sizes.

- Standard 65 by 85mm
- Narrow Standard 40 bu 85mm
- Miniature 45 by 65mm
- Midget 45 by 52mm

The movement itself is the same as any typical mechanical clock movement and is serviced in just the same way. You will note the large gearing from the spring barrel to the center wheel; this gearing must assist, to ensure the duration of going for one year, and the coarse tooth work be adequate to the strong pressure of the mainspring in the clock. Three auxiliary wheels make possible a going time of one year.

It runs much slower than the normal clock movement, at 6 to 15 beats per minute, so you will find much less wear in the parts.

For full in-depth instructions on repairing Anniversary Clocks, see

Happy Anniversary Clock?s - 400-Day Owners Repair Manual

by D. Rod Lloyd, available at

www.ClockWatchBooks.com

When a liquid boils, it expands greatly, just like steam can power a steam engine. As the bellows expand and contract, a chain winds the spring.

One degree of temperature change will wind the spring enough to run the clock for two days. When it has been running for a while, it will be fully wound and stay that way.

An Atmos Clock is

- **the Rolex of clocks**
- **the Picasso of art**
- **the Mozart of music**
- **where Science and Art meet**

They are all handmade and hand-finished, not mass-produced.

When it was invented in 1928, it was well ahead of its time. Almost a century later, it still is.

It must be precisely level, using the fitted round "bull's eye" spirit level. Better still, the pendulum pipe centered but not touching the bottom aperture. It can be fine-tuned for level with the two adjustable feet.

The Atmos clock is a torsion pendulum movement made by Jaeger-LeCoultre in Switzerland. Some consider it to be perpetual motion as it requires no winding or other means of power. The balance wheel rotates very slowly. One rotation every 30 seconds or 120 PBH [beats per hour.]

Power comes from an aneroid canister commonly and hereinafter called 'bellows' filed with Ethyl Chloride, C_2H_5Cl, which boils at 54 degrees Fahrenheit, so it is mostly in a gaseous form.

Use the minute hand to set the time, only forward as usual. Be sure the balance wheel has reached an extreme in its swing and is properly locked.

For full in-depth instructions on repairing the Atmos Clocks, see

The Atmos Repairer's Bench Manual

by D. Rod Lloyd, available at

www.ClockWatchBooks.com

The clock itself is a traditional simple one train timepiece. The clock ticks once every 30 seconds. This is sixty times slower than a traditional mechanical clock. With very little torque, there is very little friction and wear, so the clock only needs servicing when it stops working [every twenty years or more].

The escapement can be regulated using the regulation lever. It will never keep perfect time, but correctly adjusted, it should be accurate to within a minute or two a month.

Length of a Pendulum

If you buy a clock without a pendulum, you can use the following to calculate the correct length:

Tips on Counting Teeth
With a sharpie, place a dot next to the tooth that you will start counting. Now you will know when to stop counting.

If the wheel is out of the movement, run the wheel across a sheet of paper and count the holes.

Formulae:

$$BPM = \frac{W_E \times W_4 \times W_3 \times W_C}{P_E \times P_4 \times P_3} \times \frac{2}{60} \text{ [5 wheel train]}$$

OR

$$BPM = \frac{W_E \times W_3 \times W_C}{P_E \times P_3} \times \frac{2}{60} \text{ [4 wheel train]}$$

$$L_P = \frac{141120}{BPM^2}$$

where,
BPM is beats per minute
W_E is the number of teeth on the escape wheel
W_4 is the number of teeth on the fourth wheel
W_3 is the number of teeth on the third wheel
W_C is the number of teeth on the center wheel or center pinion for a 4-wheel train
P_E is the number of leaves on the escape wheel pinion
P_4 is the number of leaves on the fourth wheel pinion
P_3 is the number of leaves on the third wheel pinion
L_P is the pendulum length

Look for a number stamped on the rear plate of the movement for clues. These numbers were there to assist in making the case, not to help replace a pendulum.

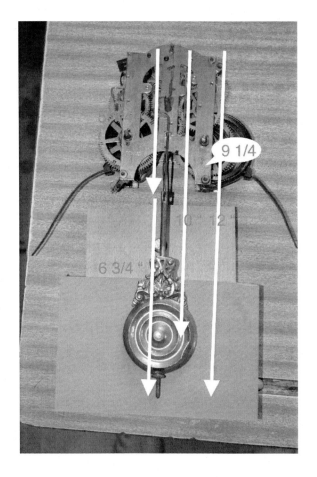

Look for clues with the clock case. Obviously, the pendulum must fit in the case with a little clearance.

Or, you can make a temporary pendulum using wire or a stick and experiment until it is approximate, then buy a pendulum that length and fine-tune it using the rating screw.

If available, try a pendulum from another similar clock.

Without going into detail about pendulum design, the standard pendulum rod will expand and contract with temperature, affecting its timekeeping. More expensive clocks have attempted to minimize this by compensating pendulums of various types.

The weight of the pendulum bob itself has little effect on the period of the pendulum. However, a heavier bob helps to keep the pendulum moving smoothly until it receives its next push from the clock's escapement mechanism. That increases the pendulum's reliability, making the motion of the pendulum more independent of the escapement and the errors it introduces, leading to increased accuracy. On the other hand, the heavier the bob is, the more energy must be supplied by the clock's power source, and more friction and wear occurs in the clock's movement. Pendulum bobs in quality clocks are usually made as heavy as the clock's movement can drive. A standard weight for the bob of a one-second pendulum, widely used in grandfather clocks and many others, is 15 lbs.

You might come across a pendulum like this one. It is called a compensating pendulum. As the temperature rises, the pendulum gets longer, but the mercury also expands, rising up the tubes at the same rate, so the center of gravity stays the same.

Missing Suspension Spring

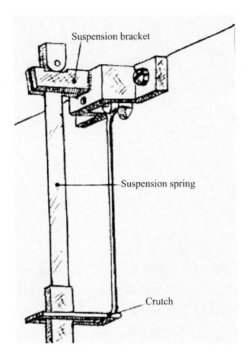

The suspension spring is the flexible transition from the static clock movement to the swinging pendulum. They come in many shapes and sizes.

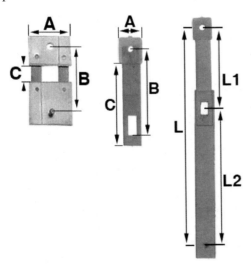

They can be obtained from the usual supply houses, but if the old one is missing, how do you know how long, wide, thick to order?

There is no easy answer. There is no such thing as a chart or book giving the proper length of suspension spring for any particular clock, or simple formula to calculate it out.

But you can use the following tips to find a suitable suspension spring.

1. Select a spring with the correct top and bottom attachment.

2. Take the mathematical length of the pendulum and deduct the actual length of the pendulum to determine the missing length. Note, the length of the pendulum is measured from the center of the pendulum bob [in most cases] to the center of the suspension spring [or point of flex].

3. Look for the marks that have been made by the crutch pin, or fork. With everything lined up you can measure, or trial fit, a suspension that will be very close to the old one. The marks will line up.

4. Buy a selection of springs. You will need them eventually.

5. A heavy pendulum needs a thicker spring; a light pendulum uses a thinner spring.

6. The inflection point is a little below the center of the spring. The lighter the spring, the more this goes lower. A thicker or wider spring would also speed up

Rule of thumb is to use as light a suspension spring as the weight of the pendulum will allow.

A heavy bob is less affected by this parameter than a light one. The inflection point of a spring can be determined by drawing a straight line along the center of the pendulum with the pendulum swung to either side.

If the pendulum does not swing in a straight line, or rolls, a new or broader spring is indicated.

When the pendulum wobbles, it is likely the suspension spring being crippled, that is, twisted, bent, or partially broken. Or it may be loose in the stud or lack of proper freedom for the pendulum wire in the crutch.

Alarm Clocks

Alarms clocks in the past were considered an inexpensive, disposable item. The cost to repair one was more than it was worth.

Today, alarms clocks are becoming collectors' items, and the owners want them repaired to running order. Many alarms clocks make good repair projects, but others are riveted together, making repairs almost impossible.

To remove the movement from the case, the winding keys are rotated in the opposite direction of winding. The hand setting and alarm knob are usually friction tight and should pull off. If it does not come off easily, wrap a cloth around it, and use pliers.

Occasionally a knob does not need to be removed at all.

Remove the case nuts and slide the case clear. If legs are fitted, they may need to be screwed off also.

Some clocks require the removal of the bezel or crystal to remove the movement. Look for tabs that fit into the side of the case. Press gently inwards. Next, remove the hands using a hand putter or prybars. Be sure to protect the dial with a slip of paper.

Often, several tabs hold the face on, and when the tabs are straightened, the face will lift off. You now have full access to the movement.

The next task is to remove the power from the springs. You will need to improvise a letdown tool. One way is to use the time side winding key and a piece of a wooden broom handle. See the previous explanation of this. You can't usually get to the alarm spring click, so set the clock so it will alarm and let it "run down" giving a little help near the end to be sure it is run down. The clock is now safe to work on.

Remove all the knobs. The springs can now be removed by removing the small screws around the spring plate, and one nut in the case of the alarm spring.

The next step takes some care, and that is removing the balance wheel. First, un-pin the hairspring, then gently rotate the balance and ease the hairspring tail out of the regulator slot. Next, unscrew the balance pivot cup on the end away from the regulator and lift out the balance using care not to tangle the hairspring on anything. It can help to clip an alligator clip on the wheel, so you don't drop it into the works.

Next, take lots of pictures! From here on, its just a matter of taking it apart, recording where everything goes, and not losing any parts. The alarm set shaft has a threaded round nut [no flats] that must be unscrewed. There should be a flat washer with a keyed hole under the nut AND another keyed flat washer just under the plate. Don't lose these, and don't forget to put all of them back.

Some movements do not have nuts, but the ends of the posts pass through the plate and are twisted. With flat pliers, push the sticking out ends of the posts together until they stand up vertically. Then the top plate can be removed. When you have it put back together, bend the sticking out post ends outwards again to secure the plate. This repair can be done only a limited number of times until the post ends break, but you should be good for several years. Just make sure that everything is in place and looks good before bending the post ends back.

Other than the above and common sense, just don't force anything. DO NOT PUT THE WHEELS [GEARS] IN AN ULTRASONIC CLEANER! The ultrasonic cleaner will eat up the soft case. The mainsprings should be removed, cleaned, and because they are narrow and relatively light, this can be done by hand.

Once it is apart and cleaned, you can evaluate what else may need to be done. It all goes back together in the reverse of how it came apart.

Most alarm clocks operate with a balance wheel and hairspring, which is more complicated than the usual escapement used in pendulum clocks. In a way, an alarm clock is like a large wristwatch and, as such, can be a good experience if you want to move on to working on watches later.

As always, be sure to make detailed sketches, photos and understand where everything belongs and what they do. Feel the amount of endshake the balance wheel has and be prepared to provide the same amount of endshake when you reassemble the movement. Remove the pin that secures the hairspring and making sure not to distort it in any way as you remove the balance wheel.

Clean the movement as usual, but the hairspring needs to be cleaned in "OneDip" available at the supply house. Polish the pivots, install any needed bushings, and reassemble the movement exactly as it was. Oil the pivots and put it back in its case.

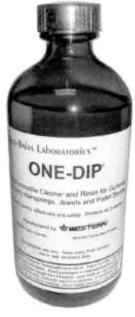

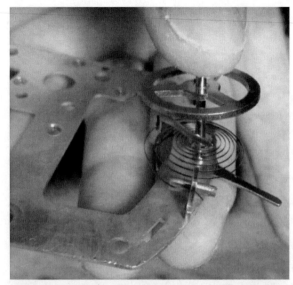

Baby Ben

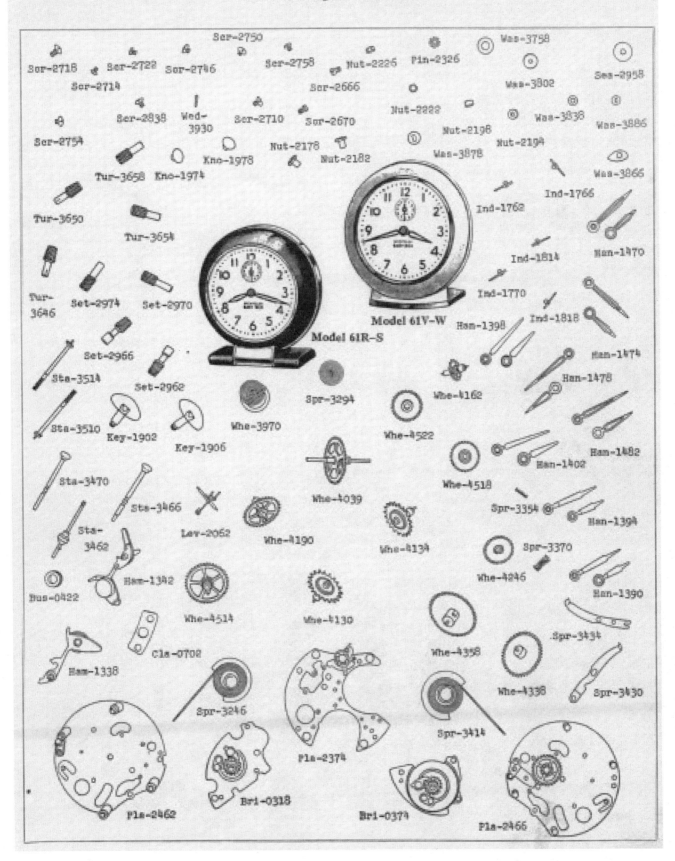

Scr-2718 Scr-2714 Scr-2722 Scr-2746 Scr-2750 Scr-2758 Nut-2226 Pin-2326 Was-3758 Was-3802 Sea-2958

Scr-2754 Scr-2838 Wed-3930 Scr-2710 Scr-2670 Scr-2666 Nut-2222 Nut-2198 Nut-2194 Was-3838 Was-3886 Was-3866

Kno-1978 Nut-2176 Nut-2182 Was-3878

Tur-3658 Kno-1974

Tur-3650

Tur-3654

Tur-3646 Set-2974 Set-2970

Set-2966

Sta-3514

Sta-3510 Key-1902 Key-1906 Whe-3970 Spr-3294 Whe-4162

Set-2962

Sta-3470

Sta-3466 Lev-2062 Whe-4190 Whe-4039 Whe-4134 Whe-4522 Whe-4518

Sta-3462 Spr-3354 Han-1394

Han-1342 Spr-3370 Whe-4246 Han-1390

Bus-0422 Whe-4514 Whe-4130 Whe-4358 Spr-3434

Han-1338 Cla-0702 Whe-4338 Spr-3430

Spr-3246 Pla-2374 Spr-3414

Pla-2462 Bri-0318 Bri-0374 Pla-2466

Model 61R-S

Model 61V-W

Ind-1762 Ind-1766 Ind-1814 Ind-1770 Ind-1818 Han-1398 Han-1470 Han-1474 Han-1478 Han-1482 Han-1402

Watches

I want to say a few words about watch repair.

By far, most hobbyists work on clocks rather than watches. It is my opinion that much more would work on watches if they had a little guidance and encouragement, so I will give a brief introduction here.

The biggest fear about watches is how small the parts are, especially for the more mature adults whose vision is less than stellar. The fact is, with the correct working environment and optical aids, all this can be easily overcome.

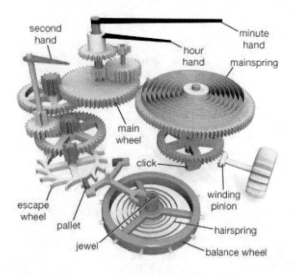

When I was at horological school, we spent time working on watches. At the start of each session, I would set up my workspace with my project and all the tools at hand, quiet with good lighting. I would sit in front of my project for a minute as an "attitude adjustment" period, slowing down my body and mind and gaining a calm peace. I would put on my optical magnification and "climb inside the movement" so to speak and work on the project.

At this point, I will point out the positives of working on watches.

- The process of working on watches is "one item at a time." Stripping down a movement means taking each part off the movement one item at a time in a logical sequence. Even watches with many "complications" [calendar, automatic action, stopwatch, etc.] just means more parts to remove in the sequence. With good notes, everything is very logical.

- The movement is basically "time only," i.e., no additional trains for striking or chiming.

- The movement is usually 30-hour, not eight days or 30 days, so there are not many wheels.

- As opposed to clocks that have one front plate and one rear plate and as many as 15 wheels and several levers must be fitted **all at the same time**, watches typically have "bridges' that often only contain one, two or three wheels, so re-assembly is a breeze.

Here you see the bridge that holds the balance wheel, held by one screw [actually called a cock], then the bridge that holds the mainspring barrel, held by two screws.

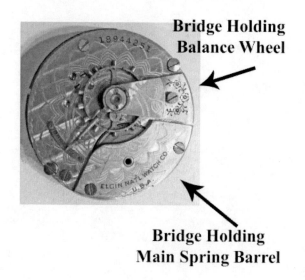

Bridge Holding Balance Wheel

Bridge Holding Main Spring Barrel

Removing the remaining train bridge held by three screws exposes the remaining three wheels.

I recommend first practicing on a pocket watch, ideally an 18 Size Railroad Style Pocket Watch Movement by Elgin. This is one of the largest watches and very easy to work on. Or better still find a "3 finger pocket watch". Each wheel has its own bridge.

There are several good videos on YouTube showing disassembly and reassembly for these watches, and you can usually find them inexpensively on eBay.

Once you have stripped, cleaned and put one back together, you will find working on all other watches is very similar and straightforward. Find a good book on watch repair like "Practical Watch Repairing" by Donald De Carl. Give it a try.

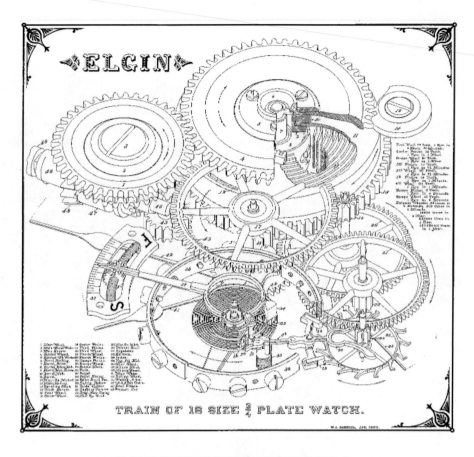

The Lathe

Why a lathe?

One of the most expensive ~~toys~~ tools we use is a jeweler's lathe. However, used lathes are often available on eBay for a few hundred dollars.

I am going to give a general description of a lathe and what it is used for.

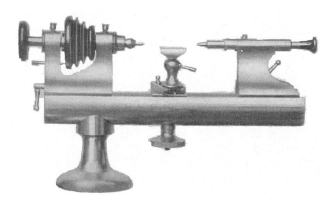

Collets come in sets, and the work is held in the collet the same size as the work it holds. This set is 3 to 80, with no gaps. A good beginner set of collets could consist of: 10, 12, 14, 16, 20, 25, 30, 35, 40, 45, 50 and this will cover most items.

It is important the correct size collet is used as described below.

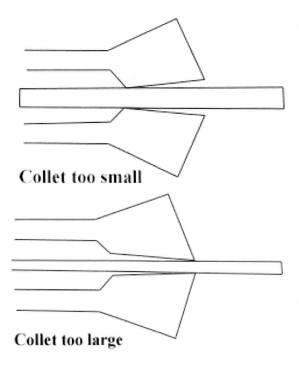

Collet too small

Collet too large

A jewelers' lathe is a small lathe suited to the clock and watch repair. It consists of a:
Bed – the general base and horizontal support
Headstock – holds and drives the work
Tailstock – can support the end of the work or hold tools
Tool rest – to support tools that do the cutting
Motor – to drive the headstock using a belt and controlled by a footswitch
Cutting tools – gravers, drills, files, etc

Lathes come in different sizes. 8mm is most common, but some use a 10mm size. The size refers to the size of the collet it takes.

The 'work' is most commonly held in a collet rather than a chuck.

The collet must be the same internal diameter as the work it holds, so it grips the work its entire length keeping the material very stable.

If the collet is too small or too large, the inside of the workpiece can be unstable and wobble, making the cut inaccurate. It might mark the work also where it grips.

It is nice to have a way to hold drill bits - either collets or small Jacobs chuck in the tailstock.

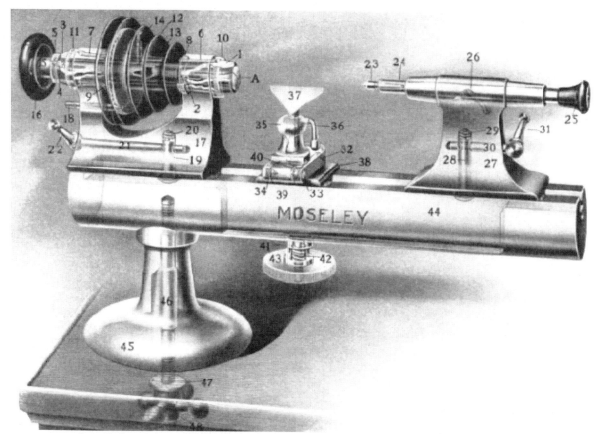

An early American-made Moseley lathe of the "WW" type with parts as annotated by the maker.

1. Headstock Spindle	2. Throat pin	3. Loose bearing	4. Loose bearing pin
5. Adjusting nut	6. Front bushing	7. Rear Bushing	8. Front inside shield
9. Rear inside shield	10. Front outside shield	11. Rear outside shield	
12. Pulley	13. Pulley Hub	14. Pulley screw	15. Draw-in spindle
16. Draw-in spindle wheel	17. Frame	18. Index pin	19. Bolt
20. Spring	21. Eccentric	22. Lever	23. Pointed Centre
24. Spindle	25. Spindle Button	26. Spindle Binder	27. Frame
28. Bolt	29. Spring	30. Eccentric	31. Lever
32. Slide	33. Pivot Screw	34. Pivot Screw	35. Post
36. Lever	37. T graver rest	38. Shoe	39. Shoe bolt

The work that can be performed by a lathe:

Polishing pivots

Pegging

Re-pivoting [broken off pivots]

Straightening bent pivots

Making replacement clock and watch parts

Make your own bushings and taper pins

Repairing parts

But the best part is you can make your own tools.

Micro Drilling

The system that I used is simple and self-explanatory in the following photos. The tailstock spindle was replaced with a mild steel spindle and fine threaded on one end [40 TPI] to hold a threaded sleeve and threaded plastic ball. Spindles for the major brands are generally 5/16" or 8MM, and stock is available from metal suppliers for about $2.00 per ft. The large round item in the photo is a 3" neoprene fender washer. It is friction fitted to the threaded spindle sleeve. Everything but the spindle stock and fine thread Taps/Dies are available at Hardware stores. The next photo shows everything assembled and ready for use.

To place in use, first spot drill, then drill a drill shank size hole in the new spindle where the drill will be inserted. This assures highly accurate drill alignment. Also, micro drills usually come in a single standard shank size for many drill sizes, such as circuit board drills as an example. As such, two or three spindles will cover most of one's needs.

In operation, you apply continual light forward pressure gripping the ball at the rear of the spindle. At the same time, you slowly rotate the 3" disc allowing the drill to slowly advance. Spot drilling before drilling and mechanical controlled feed rate is the key to protecting a drill from breakage. On items of value, especially with carbide drills, I do not advance the drill greater than the diameter of the drill every two minutes or so. Thus the 3" disc. 1500-2000 rpm should be Max.

With this setup, a person with no experience can successfully drill a hole down to about .002" [.05 mm] or about half the balance staff pivot size in the photo on their first attempt. All that is required is steady tension on the tailstock spindle and slowly rotate the 3" disc no more than a 1/4 turn every two minutes.

Clock wheels that fit into the Lathe can be drilled for pivots or whatever in the same manner per the last photo.

To protect micro drills, mount them in a collet in the lathe headstock with the shank out. Then move the tailstock spindle over the shank installing the drill. Removal is done in the same way.

The shanks on micro drills are quite long, thus the hole should also be equally deep. If quality drills are used, the hole fit to the shank will offer far more resistance than drilling these small holes.

Clock Marts

Organizations like the NAWCC hold annual marts where dozens of fellow members and clock hobbyists set out tables of clocks, practice movements, tools, books, and materials for sale at reasonable prices. A swap meet dedicated to clock repair. These sellers hold a wealth of knowledge and can be a sauce of local mentors or support. There are often classes held at the same time. Contact the NAWCC to find an upcoming local mart.

Troubleshooting

In this section, I will provide some miscellaneous problems and their solutions.

Problem getting into beat.

If you have trouble getting a movement into beat and it has a regulator, a **very slight** amount of "slop" or movement in the Chops or the part of the regulator assembly which raises or lowers the suspension spring through the chops could be the cause. The bottom line: Don't forget to evaluate the regulator assembly for wear or looseness critically. Even a very slight amount of looseness there can rob enough energy to cause seemingly random stalling problems.

Must Be Firm No Slop!

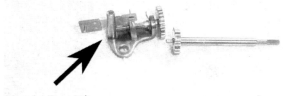

Must Be Firm
No Slop!

Slop in the pallet arbor and/or the escape wheel pivots will create some lost motion, as will excessive clearance between the crutch loop and the pendulum rod. These will reduce the pendulum arc, sometimes to the point where the clock won't run reliably or at all. Note that often pallet arbors with seemingly insignificant side-play can cause a remarkable amount of trouble; I often bush these even if they seem fine.

Lost Weights

If you have a clock without weights, one trick I learned is that you can use a fish weighing scale. You tie one side to clock cable and other side to a large weight. As the clock runs and the weight touches the floor, the clock will continue running until the scale spring stop pulling hard enough to make the clock run. When the clock stops, the scale points to the minimum weight required to run. Round up the value to make it a little more robust.

Lessons Learned

From teaching my clock repair class, I can give some feedback that many students fail to learn the first time around. I will use this feedback to provide you with a heads up and an essential recap of things to pay extra attention.

Many students seem to have a problem with the importance of pivot and pivot-hole polishing. It is vital that whenever a movement is dismantled, **ALL** the pivots and pivot holes be re-polished to a very high standard. Not just cleaned in soapy water, or even a good quality clock cleaning solution, not just making a dull pivot a little shinier. Not just removing grooves, but making the pivot very flat, smooth, and glass shiny so you can see reflections in it.

Before putting the movement back together, test each wheel **individually** between the plates to make sure it spins very freely. Then check **two wheels** together and finally the complete train [without the 1st wheel or escapement], and make sure everything runs smoothly. I have countless times tried to help a student where the clock will not run when put back together. Invariably they have not followed this procedure and must take the movement apart again to make small adjustments.

The escape wheel teeth must be in **perfect** condition for a clock to run. The slightest deviation to any tooth and the clock will stop or skip when the escapement gets to this tooth. I have yet to see a successful replacement of an escape wheel, even if the mating pallets are obtained with it.

Many students skip the step of making diagrams, especially noting the position of levers and pins. Or they lose the diagrams and or photos. It comes back to haunt them on assembly.

Clean all the parts as soon as you have dismantled the movement, but re-clean everything immediately before re-assembly, and this time do not touch the pieces with your bare hands.

Always use the correct, well-fitting screwdriver for each screw. Take pride in keeping the screws in perfect condition.

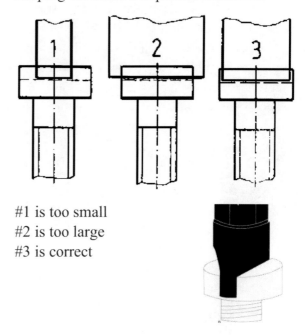

#1 is too small
#2 is too large
#3 is correct

Never, never, never open up a movement without capturing the mainspring, especially when adjusting the escapement or striking.

Clocks have only one known predator – the well-meaning hobbyists. Respect the clock, work slowly, and methodically. Use the correct tools.

Conclusion

WE NEED YOU!

Caution, clock repairing is addictive.

This introduction is just the beginning of your learning curve. Before you know it, you will be buying old clocks that don't run and making them work. You will be able to repair clocks for family and friends or even to make extra money.

If you have been following along with a project clock, you have been performing engineering at the highest level, making repairs and adjustments to 1/1,000th of an inch.

Please bear in mind, the clockmakers of the past served a five-year apprenticeship under the direction of a master clockmaker in order to learn and master the techniques, then another 5 years working for the master at fine-tuning and perfecting their skills. Then they could call themselves a Horologist. I feel privileged to work on these masterpieces. I urge you to work hard, enjoy the journey, and have fun in your apprenticeship.

You are not alone. I strongly urge you to join a local clock club i.e. NAWCC or AWCI. Attend clock marts. Watch YouTube clock videos. Buy more books. Practice, Practice, Practice.

At the very least, monitor the free message boards at
www.mb.nawcc.org
www.awci.com/forum

There are many fine historical and modern timepieces in daily use, and we need more people to service and maintain them.

Clock and Watch Associations

National Association of Watch and Clock Collectors [NAWCC]
717-684-8261
www.nawcc.org

American Watch-Clockmakers Institute [AWCI]
513-367-9800
www.awci.com

British Horological Institute [BHI]
[01636]813795
www.bhi.co.uk

Clock Supply Houses

TimeSavers [tools, parts, and supplies]
Box 12700
Scottsdale, AZ 85267
800-552-1520
480-483-3711
www.timesavers.com

S. LaRose Inc. [tools, parts, and supplies]
3223 Yanceyville St.
Greensboro, NC 27405
888-752-7673
336-621-1936
www.slarose.com

Norkro Clock Supplies [tools, parts, and supplies]
2209 NW Mill Pond Rd.
Portland, OR 97229
800-566-7576
www.norkro.com

Empire Clock [tools, parts, and supplies]
1295 Rice Street
St. Paul, MN 55117

800-333-8463
651-487-2885
www.empireclock.com

Merritts Antiques Inc. [tools, parts, and supplies]
1860 Weavertown Road
P.O. Box 277
Douglasville, PA 19518-0277
610-689-9541
www.merritts.com

Mile Hi Clock Supplies [Manufacturer of Keystone Tools and Mainspring Lubricants]
877-906-1200 Order Line
303-469-1220 Assistance
www.milehiclocksupplies.com

Butterworths clocks [supplier of Hermle, Urgos, Kieninger Herr cuckoo, etc. movements]
5300 59th. Ave. West
Muscatine, IA 52761
563-263-6759
www.buttersworthclocks.com

Meadows and Passmore
[Brighton England]
www.m-p.co.uk

Horological Tool Suppliers

Sherline Products Inc. [lathes, mills, and accessories]
3235 Executive Ridge
Vista, CA 92081-8527
800-541-0735
760-727-5857
www.sherline.com

P.P. Thornton LTD [clock wheel cutters]
The Old Bakehouse
Upper Tysoe
Warwickshire
CV35 0TR United Kingdom

TimeTrax [clock timing machines]
Can be purchased at www.merritts.com
Makers of TimeTrax www.adamsbrown.com

MicroSet [clock timing machines]
805-687-5116 www.bmumford.com

Practical Clock Repairing.... Donald DeCarle
Clock Design & Construction

Horological Book Sellers

Clock Watch Books
www.ClockWatchBooks.com

Arlington Books
http://www.arlingtonbooks.com
US Books www.usbooks.com

Recommended Books
My Clock Won?t Run….D. Rod Lloyd
The Clock Repair First Reader.... P.E. Balcomb
The Clock Repair Primer.... P.E. Balcomb
The Top 300 Trade Secrets of a Master Clockmaker. J.M. Huckabee
Clock Repair Basics.... Steven Conover
Clock Repair Skills.... Steven Conover
Chime Clock Repair.... Steven Conover
Clock Repair Tips.... B.C. Tipton

Frequently Asked Student Questions

I think I overwound the clock. It's wound all the way, and the clock won't run.

In actual fact, it is almost impossible to overwind a clock. Once the coils of a flat mainspring are in firm contact with one another, the spring cannot be physically wound any tighter. The only way to truly overwind a clock spring is to turn it so tightly that the spring actually breaks. The most likely problem is that the lubrication on the mainspring has failed due to age.

As lubricant ages, its viscosity slowly rises [it gets thicker]. Eventually, a lubricant no longer acts as a lubricant and gets tacky. This causes the coils of the mainspring to physically stick together. In actual fact, it's time for a cleaning /overhaul to remove old lubricant and accumulated dirt and replace it with fresh oil specially designed for clocks.

My clock use to run a full week on a winding, but now it will only run for a day or two.

The same answer as above. A clock that only runs a few days on a winding when it should run a week, likely has lubrication problems, although not usually the mainsprings. It is likely that the lubricant found in each bearing surface of the gears has failed and likely, there is a buildup of dirt and grime attracted by the lubricant. It is time for a cleaning. Alternatively, the spring might have become "set" or has lost its elasticity. It is time for a new spring.

My clock was just cleaned, and it won't run for more than a few minutes, even when fully wound. Also, I checked it with a level, and it is level on the wall/mantle

My first suspicion when I hear this comment is to question whether the clock is in beat. A clock being in or out of beat has nothing to do with a clock being level. First, to explain what "in beat" means. A clock is in beat when ticks and tocks occur with the same time interval between each tick and tock. You can listen to a clock's ticking and make a pretty close approximation of an "in beat" condition.

If you have trouble hearing the difference between in and out of beat, purposely tilt the clock slightly left or right off level. It's easier to hear different time intervals when the out of beat condition is exaggerated. Sometimes, a clock can be knocked out of beat by over swinging the pendulum. Also, moving a clock from one location to another without immobilizing the pendulum can knock a clock out of beat. Some wall clocks have a degree's scale attached to the clock behind the tip of the pendulum. In such cases, I will set the clock up to be in beat when the tip of the pendulum is centered on this convenient scale.

My clock stops once an hour

Does the clock stop every time the hands are overlapping? If this is the case, then the most likely cause is that the hands are interfering with one another. It could also be a striking problem.

I was winding my clock and I heard a loud bang and now the clock won't wind.

In this case, the problem is usually related to one of two possible causes. Either the mainspring has broken, or, the ratchet pawl on the mainspring has failed. The ratchet mechanism is responsible for preventing the mainspring for unwinding as you wind a clock. It is the clicking that you hear as you wind. It is important to check out the rest of the mechanism after an explosive release of a mainspring, as there is often other damage that occurs. Bent arbors and bent or missing teeth are the most common problems seen when a mainspring or ratchet fails.

I'm interested in going into the clock repair business. Where can I go to get training?

AWCI is the only establishment in the US that certifies professionals. They have home study courses, in-house training at their facility in Ohio, and professionals who travel around the country and do training. BHI, based in England, also certifies professionals and has a home study course as well as in-house training. Both institutes turn out some of the finest professionals in the business but their course studies are demanding.

The NAWCC's School of Horology is another resource for education. Although not able to professionally certify their students, it is a wonderful training ground for those interested. The school's disclaimer reads "The Avocational courses and the Specialty courses do not fall under the School's accreditation with ACCSCT. These courses are strictly taken as hobbyist courses or courses to further enhance the knowledge of people working in the industry." The NAWCC also has field suitcase courses which are organized through local NAWCC chapters around the country.

There are a number of books available if you are unable to afford to take classes and would like to be self-taught. The best books are DeCarle's "Clock Repair" and Goodrich's "The Modern Clock". These are available online from Arlington Books.

The only other way to learn the trade is to become an apprentice to a clockmaker. Ask around and see if there is anyone willing to train you but don't be disappointed if you don't find someone. Persons who are qualified to take on an apprentice, and have the time to do so, are few and far between.

How do I transport my clock?

If you're moving a clock that has a pendulum, please make sure you remove the pendulum from the clock and wrap it to keep it from damaging the movement or your case. If you cannot get the pendulum off by yourself, you can cushion and wrap it with towels or some other material to keep it from swinging wildly as you move it.

Why did my clock stop after running perfectly for so many years?

Clocks work great…until they stop. Over the years, the holes in the movement plates become worn and elongated, therefore misaligning the gears and wheels, causing the amount of force required to run the clock to be so great as to stop it. The oil dries up and becomes gummy, causing the clock to work dry and have excessive wear. Even with regular oiling, every clock will eventually wear out and stop working. Without regular oiling, they wear out even faster.

My clock is over 100 years old. Can you still get parts for it?

As you might guess, parts for antique clocks are not always available. Most clock repair shops do not have the expertise or equipment to fabricate or rebuild worn and damaged parts that were manufactured in the 18th or 19th centuries.

How do I reset my clock?

Since there are some older antique clocks whose hands cannot be turned backward, there is a common misconception that you must never turn the hands backward on any clock. It is okay to move the hands backward on all modern clocks and most antiques. If you try to move the hands backward and you feel resistance, don't force them. It is always okay to move the hands forward, waiting at each hour, ½ hour, or ¼ hour for the chimes & strikes.

Is my clock worth repairing?

I cannot answer this question specifically since each clock and clock owner is different, but I can share with you, what I feel is the best way to come to a decision.

There are two kinds of clocks we will consider here. The first type is a clock that has no emotional value to a person at all; it is simply a functioning clock that no longer works. In this case, the replacement value of the piece should factor into the decision. If the clock is going to cost as much or more to repair than it is to replace, you might as well replace it. An honest clockmaker will inform his customer when this is the case.

The other kind of clock is one that has either been passed down to its current owner through a family member, the current owner intends to pass it on to their children or the clock holds some special sentiment or meaning to the individual. In this case, the most important factor is not its replacement value, but its emotional or sentimental value. Because this type of clock is "one of a kind" and essentially irreplaceable, it is well worth whatever the cost of a proper repair would be.

Most of the time when dealing with a quality clock, even a complete overhaul of the clock movement is going to cost less than the clock's actual value. On some of the more common antique clocks, the cost will frequently come very close to or perhaps be a little more than its actual value and the more unusual or rare pieces will have a repair cost that will fall well below. Unless the clock has been purchased for "investment" reasons or for resale, the clock's emotional value should be considered first.

Should I replace my worn clock dial?

Many early American clocks had dials that were nothing more than a printed piece of paper glued to a metal dial pan. As these paper dials aged many of them have become extremely dirty and or worn badly.

Many times, the customer will ask whether anything can be done about this and if it will affect the clock's value. The first thing I do is ask them if they are planning to sell the clock. If they are not, then the value of the clock after a dial replacement is not a factor.

In the case of most common clocks, if the value of the clock is an important consideration in making the decision to replace or not, I will usually tell them that they have lost either way. If the clock's dial is in bad enough condition to consider a replacement, then some of the clock's value is lost already. Whether the dirty, badly worn dial is left in place or the dial is replaced, when it comes time to sell the clock, the purchaser will likely want to pay less either way. If the purchaser is an investment style collector he will be less interested either way because he will only be looking for clocks in original and mint condition.

Therefore, unless the clock is rare or has great antique value I tell them they should do what they think will please them the most when they look up at their clock sitting on the shelf or hanging on the wall.

Should I refinish my clock case?

The answer to this question is essentially the same as the last one. However, I'll add this. Many people now watch the "Antique Roadshow" on TV. They have heard the appraiser's comments about how a particular item's value has been diminished due to refinishing. This certainly can be true. A very rare piece is often worth more even if the original finish is in very bad condition. Notice I said very rare! Most clocks that people are bringing in for repair and considering the "refinish question" have clocks that are only worth several hundreds of dollars and although quite old are not rare at all. Frequently, the antique furniture in question on the "Antique Roadshow" is worth thousands and thousands of dollars, not a few hundred.

For most of my customers, the sentimental value far outweighs any antique value. Therefore, they are repairing, refinishing and or replacing dials for their personal satisfaction, not for some future investment return.

Each clock owner must decide this question for themselves.

How often should my clock be oiled?

Manufacturers recommend oiling every 2 to 3 years, with a professional cleaning every 5 to 7 years. To get the most years out of your clock's movement, you should follow this advice.

Why does a clock have to be cleaned and oiled?

The movement or works of a clock is a mechanical device with gears moving in contact with other gears. These gears are made of steel. These steel axles [pivots] are positioned between two brass plates. The brass plates are usually coated with lacquer to prevent oxidation [tarnish]. The holes in the brass where the steel axles rotate are NOT covered with lacquer. Tarnish will form in those areas unless protected by oil. This tarnish [oxide] breaks off in abrasive particles. It is like putting sand in a mechanical engine. These abrasive particles cause both the steel axles and the brass hole to wear out. The holes become egg-shaped, and the gears no longer mesh properly, causing

premature friction and wear. This is what kills a clock movement.

In addition, the fresh oil acts as a lubricant. The pendulum of a mechanical clock oscillates anywhere from 3,600 beats per hour to over 10,000 beats per hour. This goes on 24 hours a day, seven days a week for years. Can you imagine running your car or your sewing machine without oiling it? I have seen newer clocks be completely shot in 17 years without oiling. Older clocks will last longer due to thicker brass plates. At any rate, it appears that with proper oiling and cleaning the clock movement will last for 10 additional years or more.

Cuckoo Clock Questions

How do I set the time? It strikes 4 times on the half hour and once on the hour, and the time is not set right, and the hour hand is wrong.

Assume your clock is right and your hands are wrong. At least 90% of all cuckoo minute hands have a large round hole in them. If you get the hand off and it has a square hole in it just remove the hand and replace it in the next quarter or half hour. For the majority that does have the large round hole in them here is what you do. All the real adjustment takes place with the minute hand. Loosen the nut and remove the minute hand.

Stuck on the hand is a round piece of brass called a hand bushing. It has a square hole in it. This piece of brass needs to be turned one direction or the other and then just set the hand back on the clock. If it looks about right, put the nut on and tighten it and rotate the hand clockwise to see if it strikes the hour and half hour at the correct time. It probably won't be quite right the first time around. It rarely is for me. Be patient, adjust again.

Hold the minute hand still while you tighten the nut with a pair of pliers in the other hand. Once you get the minute hand striking where you want it to, then just move the hour hand to the last hours struck. The hour hand is a press on fit. Just turn it in either direction, then use your thumbnails to push down on each side of the hand near the shaft.

My clock runs for 3 or 4 minutes and then stops. What do I do?

First, make sure the clock is level on the wall. If it still doesn't run move the base slightly to the left and listen for an even tic-tic sound. Try running it again and if it still doesn't run move it slightly more to the left. If the tics don't even out and the clock still doesn't run then go back to level and repeat all the above by moving it to the right. Don't worry if the clock looks a little off level, right now we are trying to see if it will run. It may be out of beat and still be able to run. You won't know unless you try this first.

My chain has come off the gear. What do I do?

First, we want to avoid the other chains coming off while you are fixing this one. Take a twist tie or a piece of string and capture the other chains together right at the base of the clock. Put the twist tie or string inside the links and tie it. If you put it around the chain, they sometimes slip down the chain. This will keep those chains from coming off.

Now take the back off the clock and turn the clock upside down and give the loose chain a little slack. What you are trying to do is allowing enough slack to make a loop that you can hook around the gear sprocket.

It may take a few tries, but if you can see it, there is a good chance you can do it. Use plenty of light. Some clocks have more room in them than others. If you succeed hold onto the chain while you upright the clock. Hang it on the wall and then remove the ties on the other chains.

My clock runs and keeps time, but the cuckoo bird won't come out?

Check and see if the shipping latch above the cuckoo door is open so the door will operate freely. If the clock is new or has been shipped back to you be sure you have removed the clips that hold the bellows together. Newer cuckoos may have a night shutoff feature. Some have a shut-off lever coming out of the side or a black heavy wire with a loop on it that comes out of the bottom of the clock. Move the lever down or pull the loop down and try the cuckooing again.

I've been told by others that my movement is worn out and needs replacing. Is that the only answer and how can I tell the difference?

Here is how to tell if your clock has significant wear that is causing it to stop running or cuckooing. Caution: do not lay the clock on its back or turn it over because the chains are only held on their sprockets by gravity and will come off. While looking in the back, pull up and down on one chain. In other words tug back and forth on the winding chain and the weight chain of one wheel.

Watch the back plate where the pivots come through the plate. Particularly the 2nd gear up from the bottom. If that steel pivot rod is jumping back and forth in the hole then you have significant wear.

Keep doing it and look at the other holes as you go up each train as you are pulling. If your case is big enough to get your hand in there just wiggle the bottom gear that the chain rides on. You will get the same effect.

Usually, the wear starts on that second gear but it is normal to have 2 or 3 gears worn that much on a clock that has been run a lot. The wear causes the gears to start separating and they don't mesh well. That causes it to lose power all the way up the train of gears. Try the time side also to check for wear. If one side is worn, it is likely that the other side isn't far behind.

How does the clock operate the music box?

Notice, this is for information only, pretty please don't try to fix this yourself or you will need me or someone else for sure. I always advise people to stay away from these and don't bend anything, but some are going to anyway and at least this gives them some idea of how they work. I'm going to try to tell you how the music box works. It may not be exactly what you have, but all are similar and will give you somewhere to start. There should be 2 connections from the movement to the music box. On some movements, both wires come from the same spot. On others, there is a flat strip of metal coming from the right-hand corner of the clock and a straight wire coming off the back center of the clock.

The flat strip of metal is hooked to a linkage that pulls a locking pin out of the music box at the top of the hour.

The music box tries to play but the fan is immediately stopped by the straight wire coming off the back of the clock. That wire will move back and forth as the clock cuckoos and when it finishes it is supposed to drop away just enough to let the fan rotate freely and the music will play and will lock itself back down. That is how it is supposed to work. Getting it to do that is extremely tricky. I sometimes spend as much as a whole day on adjusting one music box. Others may take me 10 minutes. There is only one sweet spot where everything will work.

Glossary of Clock Terms

A collection of meanings of common clock terms.

Alarm

Sound a clock makes to awaken the sleeper at a certain time. They come in various sounds: bell, double bell, chirp, beep, buzz, melody, etc.

Analog

The traditional look of time told by the angular positioning of hands on a dial.

Anniversary Clock

The name comes from the fact that when it was first invented, it needed winding just once a year on its anniversary [approximately 400 days]. Characterized by a glass dome and a rotating pendulum. Also known as a "400 Day Clock".

Arabic Numerals

Most common number style [1, 2, 3, 4, etc.] used on clock dials.

Arch

The curved part of a clock case that resembles a door arch.

Beat

Term to describe the tick-tock of a mechanical timepiece. A clock is said to be in beat if the spacing between the tick and the tock are equal. If they are not equally spaced, the clock is out of beat and will generally stop after a short run.

Beveled Glass

Glass used in the clock case with an angled surface beginning about 3/4" from the edge.

Big Ben Gong

The deep-sounding chime that announces the hour. Modeled after the large bell clock in the tower of the House of Parliament in London.

Bim-Bam

Chime which only counts the hour and announces the half-hour.

Bob

Round, weighted end of a clock pendulum. Often made of brass.

Bow Top

A decorative feature found in certain mantel and wood case wall clocks. Characterized by a curved top section.

Bracket Clock

A term used by the British to indicate a table or shelf clock. Characterized by a square case with a handle on top, as it was designed to be carried from room to room.

Balloon Clock

Mantel or tabletop clocks shaped like hot-air balloons of the late 18th Century.

Burl

The decorative pattern in the wood grain caused by a series of irregularities that add to the character of the wood.

Cable Driven

Mechanical movement powered by weights hanging on cables wound with a key or crank.

Case/Cabinet

That which contains the clock, the housing or containment for the works [movement]

Carriage Clock

Small portable clock, usually has a brass case with glass sides and a decorative handle on top.

Center Shaft

The shaft that the minute hand is attached to, geared to make one revolution every 60 minutes.

Chain Driven

See also Weight Driven

Traditional cuckoo clock movement. It is driven by weights hung from chains with engaged sprockets.

Chapter Ring

A decorative ring on the clock dial upon which the hours are indicated. A feature of many traditional style mantel clocks. Also a prominent feature of clocks with skeleton movements.

Chime Melody

Tune played by the clock on the hour. A 4/4 Chime plays music and counts the hour, quarter hour, half hour, & three-quarter hour.

Chime Rods

Tuned rods which, when struck by small hammers powered by the clock movement, produce the chime melody and strike the hour. A component found in mechanical chime mantel and wall clocks.

Chip

Small silicon square onto which integrated circuits are imprinted. An integral part of the quartz movement.

Cornice

Topmost molding of a clock case. The 833-W is a great example of a well-defined cornice.

Crystal

A flat or convex piece of glass that covers the dial. Usually fitted into a brass bezel.

Day Ring

Divided ring on a lunar dial that indicates the days in the 29 1/2 day lunar cycle.

Dial

The face of a clock on which the hours are located.

Digital

Time display that uses no hands but shows the time in numbers and readout screen.

Drop Case

Wall clock with a lower case, which usually houses a swinging pendulum such as a Schoolhouse style clock.

Escapement

A means by which the pendulum allows the going train to operate at a regular interval, thus controlling the passage of time. It usually consists of anchor and escape wheel.

Etching

A process used to create a design in metal by the action of an acid. A feature found on the metal dials of many German Anniversary Clocks.

Finial

The spires, turnings, or decorative points on top of a clock case. Maybe wood or metal. Sometimes removable. Some are called "ball and spike", "urn", "acorn", etc.

Finish

Process and materials used to create an attractive wood surface. Examples include deep cherry, medium oak, mahogany, antique walnut, etc.

Grandfather Clock

The correct name is Long Case Clock [in Britain] or Tall Case Clock in the USA.

Hands

Used to mark hours, minutes, or seconds on a clock dial. Made of metal or plastic.

Inlay

Thin layers of wood applied to form a decorative pattern.

Keywound

A spring-driven clock that is wound with a key or crank.

Liquid Crystal Display [LCD]

Most frequently used in quartz alarms. Time is continuous, displayed in digital form.

Light Emitting Mode [LED]

Number telling the hours and minutes light up on a readout screen.

Lunar Dial

See also Moon Dial

An additional dial on a clock face that indicates the phase of the Moon each day.

Lyre

Ornamental feature on a pendulum resembling the ancient Greek instrument.

Marquetry

A type of decoration on wood made by inlaying wood veneers in elaborate designs.

Minute Track

Square or circular track divided into 60 equal segments. It may appear on the outer perimeter of the dial or in the dial center.

Moon Dial

See also Lunar Dial

An additional dial on a clock face that indicates the phase of the Moon each day.

Movement

Timekeeping mechanism of the clock, which also produces the strike and chime. Comes in quartz [battery], keywound, or weight-driven.

Pediment

The decorative top of a case, above the cornice.

Pendulum

A suspended, swinging rod and weight [bob] that regulates the clock movement in keywound/mechanical clocks. The pendulum in quartz [battery] clocks is purely decorative; the clock does not need it to properly function.

Pilaster

Decorative feature used to create the effect of columns on the clock cabinet.

Pinch-Waisted

Traditional clock style with the crown and case wider than the part of the clock enclosing the pendulum.

Quartz

Electronic transistorized movements that work on battery energy and require no winding or plug-in electricity. A tiny quartz crystal, vibrating at a high frequency, allows the clock mechanism to perform with extraordinary precision.

"R-A" Regulator

Slang term for wall regulator with "R-A" on the pendulum. "R" stands for retard by turning the adjusting nut toward R to lower the pendulum bob. "A" stands for advanced by turning the adjusting nut toward A to raise the pendulum bob.

Regulator

The mechanism that can be adjusted to make the clock more accurate. Sometimes the word "Regulator" is printed on the clock's glass, usually on Schoolhouse clocks.

Roman Dial

A dial with Roman numerals [I, II, III] frequently used in traditional style carriage, mantel, wall, tabletop, and anniversary clocks.

Rotating Pendulum

A feature found on both key-wound and quartz [battery] anniversary clocks. Characterized by decorative balls in crystal or metal finish.

Schoolhouse Clock

Traditional wood cabinet wall clock with a round or octagonal clock case and lower pendulum cabinet. Said to be true Early American Design. This style was most commonly found on classroom walls in American Colonial days.

St. Michael Chimes

Chimes originally installed in the St. Michael church steeple in Charleston, SC in 1764.

Scroll

A decorative ornament resembling a partially rolled scroll of paper.

Straight Sided

A style of clock cabinet in the same width from crown to base.

Strike

Chime or gong that indicates the hour.

Tambour

Style of clock case sometimes referred to as "Napoleon's Hat".

Tempus Fugit

Latin phrase meaning, "Time Flies". Sometimes engraved on a decorative panel on the clock dial or a plaque attached to the clock case.

Time train

The series of gears in the clock movement that operates the minute and hour hands [and second hand where applicable]. The time-train is responsible for activating the chime in the movement.

Triple Chimes

Movement that plays 3 different chimes: Westminster, Whittington, St. Michael

Tubular Bell Chime

Long hollow tubes which, when struck by small hammers powered by the clock movement, produce the chime melody and strike the hour.

Verge

An escapement belonging to the Foliot and Verge. Not all escapements are verges.

Veneers

Thin layers of wood chosen for their attractive grain and permanently applied to a core material. The same material and method are used in making violin and guitar cases.

Weight Driven

See also Chain Driven

Traditional cuckoo clock movement. It is driven by weights hung from chains with engaged sprockets.

Westminster Chimes

The most popular tune used in chiming clocks. This famous tune originated in the Victorian clock towers in the House of Parliament in London.

Whittington Chimes

Chimes originally rang in the church of St. Mary Le Bow in London. Legend has it that a young boy running away from his master thought he heard them call out his name, telling him to turn back. Dick Whittington did and eventually became the Lord Mayor of London.

Made in United States
North Haven, CT
18 August 2024

56238952R00128